Elegant Jeremiahs

The Aesthetic and Critical Theories of John Ruskin (1971)

Approaches to Victorian Autobiography (Editor) (1979)

William Holman Hunt and Typological Symbolism (1979)

Victorian Types, Victorian Shadows: Biblical Typology in Victorian Literature, Art, and Thought (1980)

Images of Crisis: Literary Iconology, 1750 to the Present (1982)

Ruskin (1985)

A Pre-Raphaelite Friendship: The Correspondence of William Holman Hunt and John Lucas Tupper (Co-editor with James H. Coombs, Anne M. Scott, and Arnold A. Sanders) (1986)

Elegant Jeremiahs

The Sage from Carlyle to Mailer

GEORGE P. LANDOW

Cornell University Press

ITHACA AND LONDON

First published 1986 by Cornell University Press.
Quotations from *Of a Fire on the Moon* by Norman Mailer,
copyright © 1969, 1970 by Norman Mailer.

International Standard Book Number 0–8014–1905–0
Library of Congress Catalog Card Number 86–47644
Printed in the United States of America
*Librarians: Library of Congress cataloging information
appears on the last page of the book.*

*The paper in this book is acid-free and meets the guidelines for permanence
and durability of the Committee on Production Guidelines for Book Longevity
of the Council on Library Resources.*

*For my sister Marcia Landow Silverstein,
who introduced me to the works of
Tom Wolfe and Joan Didion*

Contents

self fortunate to have the opportunity of sharing them with colleagues at various universities. I particularly thank the universities of Minnesota, New Mexico, Michigan, and Kentucky as well as Oxford and Yale universities for inviting me to share my ideas in lectures at their institutions. I owe a special debt of thanks to my sister, Marcia Landow Silverstein, to whom this volume is dedicated, for handing me a copy of Tom Wolfe's *Kandy-Colored Tangerine-Flake Streamline Baby* shortly after its publication with the direction, "Read this, you'll really like it." Neither of us thought for a moment that Wolfe would eventually appear in the company of Carlyle, Ruskin, and other earnest Victorians. My students at Brown University, who in an important sense prompted the development of the ideas contained in my book, deserve my thanks. Michael Macrone, Bruce Redford, Catherine Reed, and Paul Stark stand out as some of the very finest of these students, and although I finally did not adopt Mr. Stark's neologism *sagistic* as a much-needed term—my good friend David DeLaura found it too ugly a word and my wife complained it too closely resembled *sadistic*—I am nonetheless grateful for his suggestion. I also thank for their encouragement, criticism, and assistance Harry Ausmus, Morton Bloomfield, John L. Bradley, Patrick Brantlinger, Stephen Brook, David J. DeLaura, Ernest Frerichs, Robert Hewison, E. D. H. Johnson, Paul Sawyer, R. H. Super, and Frank Turner. I thank my wife, Ruth M. Landow, for her invaluable assistance, and I am especially grateful to Arden Reed, whose generous, detailed criticisms of an earlier version of this work did much to improve its rigor and effectiveness. Kay Scheuer of Cornell University Press copy edited the manuscript with marvelous skill, and I thank her for her efforts.

This book was written on the Brown University Computer system using its version of University of Waterloo-IBM Script, and I am grateful both to my department for funding the cost of computer time and to all those who have helped me to use (and enjoy using) the University system. In particular, I thank Lydia Colbert for helping in times of crisis and Richard A. Damon III of User Services for advice and for making the Computer Center's Xerox 9700 Electronic Printing System (laser printer) produce such beautiful output. Like all members of my depart-

10

ment who use the University system, I am grateful to James Coombs, who set up and maintained the English Department's word-processing programs as only a Miltonist could. Once again I owe a debt of gratitude to Allen H. Renear, who typeset this book on the Brown University computing system directly from my original files, for his willingness to undertake yet another such project with me—and for his unshakable good humor, logical mind, and generosity with his time.

I completed the writing of this book with the assistance of a National Endowment for the Humanities Summer Grant, and I thank this federal agency for its assistance, as I do Little, Brown and Company for granting permission to quote passages from Norman Mailer's *Of a Fire on the Moon*.

GEORGE P. LANDOW

Providence, Rhode Island

Works Frequently Cited

Quotations of individual works are taken from the following editions and collections, cited parenthetically in my text by page number and by volume number where necessary.

Matthew Arnold. *Complete Prose Works*. Edited by R. H. Super. 11 vols. Ann Arbor, University of Michigan Press, 1960–77.

Thomas Carlyle. *The Works*. Centenary Edition. Edited by H. D. Traill. 30 vols. London, Chapman and Hall, 1896–99.

Joan Didion. *Slouching towards Bethlehem*. New York, Delta Books, 1968.

———. *The White Album*. New York, Simon and Schuster, 1979.

Ralph Waldo Emerson. *Essays and Lectures*. The Library of America. Edited by Joel Porte. New York, Viking, 1983.

Norman Mailer. *Of a Fire on the Moon*. Boston, Little, Brown, 1971.

John Ruskin. *The Works*. The Library Edition. Edited by E. T. Cook and Alexander Wedderburn. 39 vols. London, George Allen, 1903–12.

Henry David Thoreau. *Reform Papers*. Edited by Wendell Glick. Princeton, N.J., Princeton University Press, 1973.

Elegant Jeremiahs

Introduction: The Genre of the Sage

In the introduction to *Culture and Anarchy*, Matthew Arnold
wryly complained that a newspaper had labeled him "an elegant
Jeremiah."[1] Although Arnold may not have been pleased that
the *Daily Telegraph* placed him in company with the Old Testament prophet, its remark does indicate that Arnold's Victorian
readers perceived his obvious relation to an ancient literary tradition—one, to be sure, whose zeal and self-proclamation made
the urbane, gentlemanly Arnold feel more than a little ill at
ease, however much he drew upon it. Readers of Carlyle and
Ruskin similarly perceived these authors' obvious indebtedness to
Jeremiah, Isaiah, Daniel, and other Old Testament prophets.
Walt Whitman, for example, commented that "Carlyle was indeed, as Froude terms him, one of those far-off Hebraic utterers,
a new Micah or Habbakuk [sic]. His words at times bubble forth
with abysmic inspiration," and he approvingly quotes Froude's description of Carlyle as "a prophet, in the Jewish sense of the

[1] Arnold remarked that for his "indifference to direct political action I have
been taken to task by the *Daily Telegraph*, coupled, by a strange perversity of
fate, with just that very one of the Hebrew prophets whose style I admire the
least, and called 'an elegant Jeremiah'" (5.88).

17

word," one of those, like Isaiah and Jeremiah, who have "interpreted correctly the signs of their own times."[2] All three Victorians in fact owed more than just their tone and their willingness to castigate their contemporaries to Old Testament prophecy, a scriptural genre that devotes itself as much to diagnosing the spiritual condition of an age as to predicting the future.

Recognizing the specific elements of Old Testament prophecy that the Victorian sages drew upon helps define the genre they created, and such definition is a crucial step in understanding this major strain in Anglo-American nonfiction. Indeed, one of the most useful approaches to the Victorian sage begins in the recognition that his writings and those of his modern heirs form a clearly identifiable genre, the definition of which offers readers crucial assistance since genre determines the rules by which one reads, interprets, and experiences individual works of literature. As Alastair Fowler has pointed out, "Traditional genres and modes, far from being mere classificatory devices, serve primarily to enable the reader to share types of meaning." In other words, the reader's understanding is "genre-bound: he can only think sensibly of *Oedipus Tyrannus* as a tragedy, related to other tragedies. If he ignores or despises genre, or gets it wrong, misreading results."[3] A good many of the problems twentieth-century readers have had with the writings of the Victorian sages derive, I suspect, from precisely such ignorance of genre and a consequent failure to recognize those signals it directs at them. Therefore, if we can determine the particular techniques that define the genre created by the writings of the sages, we can also learn how better to read the works of Carlyle, Arnold, Ruskin, and their heirs.

[2]*Specimen Days*, in *Complete Poetry and Collected Prose*, ed. Justin Kaplan (New York, Viking, 1982), pp. 898, 893.

[3]"The Life and Death of Literary Forms," in *New Directions in Literary History*, ed. Ralph Cohen (London, Routledge & Kegan Paul, 1974), p. 79. According to Fowler, "Johnson's blunder over *Lycidas* and the more recent and even more spectacular critical error of taking *Paradise Lost* as classical epic with Satan the hero are dreadful examples. Clearly, generic forms must rank among the most important of the signal systems that communicate a literary work" (79).

18

Recent years have seen a significant increase in attention paid to Victorian nonfiction as literature. In particular, the individual essays in George Levine and Lionel Madden's *Art of Victorian Prose* (1968) have done much to advance our understanding of the form, as have such book-length studies of individual authors as G. B. Tennyson's *Sartor Called Resartus* (1965), Albert J. La-Valley's *Carlyle and the Idea of the Modern* (1968), Richard L. Stein's *Ritual of Interpretation* (1975), and Elizabeth K. Helsinger's *Ruskin and the Art of the Beholder* (1982). Thus far, the best discussions of Victorian nonfiction as imaginative literature have taken two forms—those, such as George Levine's *Boundaries of Fiction: Carlyle, Macaulay, Newman* (1968), that place it in the context of the novel and those, such as Pierre Fontenay's "Ruskin and Paradise Regained"[4] and other works listed above, that place passages from individual works in the context provided by mythological and iconological studies.

John Holloway's pioneering *The Victorian Sage: Studies in Argument* (1953), which discusses Carlyle, Disraeli, George Eliot, Newman, Arnold, and Hardy, obviously places Carlyle and Arnold—it omits Ruskin—in the context of the novel and, despite its many suggestive hints and comments about the sage's nonlogical form of argumentation, in practice concentrates almost exclusively upon skillful New Critical examinations of imagery. By directing his readers' attention to how various Victorian writers of nonfiction as well as fiction attempt to convince their audiences by literary, nonlogical means, Holloway has put all subsequent students of related forms of prose in his debt. *The Victorian Sage* asks the central, the essential questions, and it has assisted many in reading works of Carlyle and Arnold as literature.

Unfortunately, despite the fact that its consideration of Carlyle, Disraeli, Eliot, Newman, Arnold, and Hardy as Victorian sages points out some interesting similarities, it finds no essential difference between novel and nonfiction. Although such an approach strikes a blow against the traditional denigration of nonfiction when contrasted to fiction, it neither directs the reader's attention toward the particular excellences of nonfiction nor

---

[4]*Victorian Studies* 12 (1969): 347–56.

provides any means of distinguishing it from fiction. Treating nonfiction as a poorer relation of fiction has its obvious polemical advantages, but it does not advance the reader's understanding of nonfiction and tends to hinder it in the long run. In fact, the situation of nonfiction in today's criticism much resembles that of painting in sister-arts criticism of the eighteenth century: In their attempt to raise the prestige of painting and make it one of the liberal arts, critics like DuFresnoy and Dryden closely allied it to literature. Unfortunately, once seventeenth- and eighteenth-century critics had convinced one another and their audiences that painting resembled poetry in all essential matters, they found themselves without any means of effectively discussing the unique strengths and beauties of the visual arts. In like manner, placing together the novel and the writings of the sage—say, *Middlemarch* and *Culture and Anarchy*, *Coningsby* and *Past and Present*—may encourage serious consideration of Arnold and Carlyle but does not offer a specific enough means of carrying it out. In its concentration upon imagery, *The Victorian Sage* does not help us perceive what is unique about the form of literature they developed. Similarly, just as putting the writings of the sage together with the productions of novelists does not much help our appreciation of the former, neither does considering them in the context of writings on history, another popular approach.

A major benefit of generic theory lies in the fact that it enables one to perceive connections and continuities within a body of works, including those not usually considered as obviously having much in common. Such theory can thereby not only encourage us to discern new relations among individual works but also enable us to redefine literary traditions and to reconceive widely accepted notions of historical development. This approach to the sage, for example, reveals links between Victorian and modern examples of this genre. Asserting a generic connection between the works of, say, Carlyle and Mailer or Ruskin and Didion might at first seem strange. One cannot, however, reject it out of hand on the basis of the assertion once made to me that Carlyle, Ruskin, and Arnold are major authors, members of the canon, whereas Mailer, Didion, Wolfe, and other moderns are journalists. In fact, those who I suggest might be twentieth-century heirs of the Victorian sages publish much of their writings in intellectual periodicals that are counterparts of the ones in which "Signs of the Times" and *Unto This Last* first appeared.

One matter does link Victorian and more recent instances of this form—both have been treated as adjuncts to fiction. The most serious critical consideration Didion and Mailer have received has come under the rubric of the New Journalism, a term invented by Tom Wolfe, who claims that the kind of nonfiction that he, Capote, and others write employs the techniques of fiction and is therefore best understood in these terms.[5] In other words, the critical situation with the best nonfiction of the past few decades is much the same we have already observed in relation to Holloway's *The Victorian Sage*—it has benefited to a large extent from being considered in relation to fiction, but at the same time some of its distinguishing qualities have necessarily been overlooked. Of course, I in no way want to deny the obvious validity of claims that in both the nineteenth and twentieth century nonfiction draws upon the novel. In fact, Carlyle and Ruskin employ invented characters, dialogue, setting, imagery, leitmotifs, and other literary techniques thought limited to the novel. Tom Wolfe, one of the contemporary American masters of nonfiction who has important things to say about the kind of work he has created, correctly points to the role played by fictional techniques in his work and that of creators of New Journalism.

I do not wish to suggest that all works considered instances of New Journalism, or even all works by Didion, Mailer, and Wolfe (or of nineteenth-century nonfiction) exemplify the writings of the sage. Many of Wolfe's most effective pieces, including the major portion of *The Pump House Gang*, devote themselves so largely to satire that they do not fit into this genre. Those works of contemporary nonfiction that do fit, however, benefit more from being considered within the tradition of the sage than

---

[5]*The New Journalism, with an Anthology*, ed. Tom Wolfe and E. W. Johnson (New York, Harper & Row, 1973). See also Ronald Weber, *The Literature of Fact: Literary Nonfiction in American Writing* (Athens, Ohio University Press, 1980), pp. 16–21.

within that of fiction. Even other forms of nonfiction, such as autobiography, may benefit from such rhetorical analyses and from such placement alongside another tradition.

A generic description of the works of the sage offers several attractive possibilities, the first and most important of which is that it promises to provide a method of studying nonfiction as literature and not just as data for the study of the history of ideas and as the cultural background for other literary forms. Second, placing this prose within the context of biblical, oratorical, and satirical traditions provides a means of relating it to earlier genres and modes, just as it also suggests an obvious way of relating its major nineteenth-century practitioners in England and America to one another and to their twentieth-century heirs. Third, it offers the possibility of finding a means, which does not depend solely upon ideology, of evaluating discursive prose.

One begins the definition by recognizing that although the pronouncements of the sage, like those of the Old Testament prophet, share some characteristic assumptions with traditional wisdom literature, they differ at one crucial point. As Morton Bloomfield has pointed out, nearly all cultures "have praised and elevated wisdom," and "perhaps the only subject which is universally admired is wisdom—not only in the Bible, or by the Greeks, but among the Hindus and Japanese, the Polynesians and the American Indians, the Hausa and the Xhosa, peoples of Africa. All peoples with few apparent exceptions admire wisdom, hypostatize and personify it, practice or say they practice it, teach it to their children, and use it to face or smooth away the irritations and dangers of everyday life."[6] Like the writings of the sage, wisdom literature solaces and aids men and women in difficult times because it rests on the assumption that the world, no matter how difficult a place in which to live, has meaning and order. Indeed, as Bloomfield reminds us, "Practical wisdom rests upon a sapiential view of the world, the view that the world makes sense, possesses order, rules and patterns to which individuals if they wish happiness must conform, and that every-

---

[6]*The Wisdom Tradition* (Seijo University, Japan, n.d.), p. 2. The passage quoted below appears on p. 3. See also Robert Preyer, "Victorian Wisdom Literature," *Victorian Studies* 6 (1962–63): 245–62.

thing and every event has its proper place and time." Thus far, traditional statements of wisdom and the writings of the sage—the Book of Proverbs and the Book of Jeremiah, for example—coincide. They differ at one crucial point, crucial because it motivates the entire genre we are considering: Whereas the pronouncements of traditional wisdom literature always take as their point of departure the assumption that they embody the accepted, received wisdom of an entire society, the pronouncements of the biblical prophet and Victorian sage begin with the assumption that, however traditional their messages may once have been, they are now forgotten or actively opposed by society. In other words, the style, tone, and general presentation of the wisdom speaker derive from the fact that his often anonymous voice resides at a societal and cultural center; it purports to be the voice of society speaking its essential beliefs and assumptions. In contrast, the style, tone, and general presentation of the sage derive from the fact that his voice resides at the periphery; it is, to use a Ruskinian etymological reminder, an eccentric voice, one off center. We might hold that wisdom literature consists of the statements of orthodoxy and the sage's writings of criticisms of that orthodoxy, except for the fact that the sage's attacks upon established political, moral, and spiritual powers often charge that they have abandoned orthodox wisdom or reduced it to an empty husk.[7] When a people can no longer follow its own wisdom literature, then it needs the writings of the sage. When a people ignores the wisdom that lies at the heart of its society and institutions, then the sage recalls that people to it.

Coleridge's fable of the maddening rain in the first essay of *The Friend* (1818) shows some of the difficulties faced by one who would recall his fellows to forgotten truths. During the golden age when men lived much closer to perfection than they do now, an elder reported to his fellows that a heavenly voice had

---

[7]See Robert Gordis, "The Social Background of Wisdom Literature," in his *Poets, Prophets, and Sages: Essays in Biblical Interpretation* (Bloomington, Indiana University Press, 1971), p. 162. Gordis, who points to the essentially conservative nature of Hebrew wisdom literature, argues that it "was fundamentally the product of the upper classes in society, who lived principally in the capital, Jerusalem."

23

warned him that soon a heavy rain would fall and "whomever that rain wetteth, on him, yea, on him and on his children's children will fall—the spirit of Madness." Ignored by all, the inspired one took shelter in a cave and emerged, horrified, to find a fallen world from which all community, honor, freedom, and sanity had vanished. Soon he was set upon by several persons who accused him of being "a worthless idler" and "a very dangerous madman" until, "harrassed [sic], endangered, solitary," he escaped from the isolation of sanity by plunging into the maddening liquid.[8] The sage, in contrast, is one who refuses to drink the maddening rain and continually tries to recall his fellows to wisdom and sanity; to do so he must stand apart from them, criticizing what they do.

Carlyle and other Victorian sages did not have to create entirely *ex nihilo* the literary devices with which they carried out this project, since they had the powerful example of the Hebrew prophets. Standing apart from society and charging its members with having abandoned the ways of God and truth had always been the function of Old Testament prophets, and nineteenth-century students of Scripture of all denominations recognized this fact. As the English Evangelical Thomas Scott pointed out in a Bible commentary that remained popular throughout much of the nineteenth century, the Old Testament prophets "were, in general, extraordinary instructors, sometimes in aid of the priests and Levites; but more commonly to supply their defects, when they neglected their duty."[9] Furthermore, according to Scott, these Old Testament prophets "were also bold reformers, and reprovers of idolatry, iniquity, and hypocrisy; they called the at-

---

[8] *The Friend* in Coleridge, *Collected Works*, vol. 4, pt. 1, ed. Barbara E. Rooke (London, Routledge & Kegan Paul, 1969; and Princeton, Princeton University Press, 1969), pp. 8–9. In the notes the editor offers several sources for the fable of the rain.

[9] *A Commentary on the Holy Bible, Containing the Old and New Testaments . . .*, 5 vols. (Philadelphia, William S. and Alfred Martien, 1858), 3: 79. Subsequent quotations from Scott in this paragraph are taken from this same page. Another representative view of Old Testament prophecy can be found in Thomas Hartwell Horne, *An Introduction to the Critical Study and Knowledge of the Holy Scriptures*, 4 vols. (London, T. Cadell, 1834), the standard work on the Bible for ministerial students of most Protestant denominations. See especially 1: 272–332; 2: 534–48; 4: 140–56.

tention of the people to the law of Moses, especially the moral law, the standard of true holiness; they shewed the inefficacy of ceremonial observances, without the obedience of faith and love." In other words, they offered no essentially new message: "The prophets did not teach any new doctrines, commands, or ordinances, but appealed to the authenticated records." Scott's description of the Old Testament prophet who unexpectedly comes forth to instruct his fellows on their spiritual and moral failings in order to help his nation survive applies to the Victorian sage in every respect but one—Scott's Evangelical emphasis that these figures from the Old Testament also "kept up and encouraged the expectation of the promised Messiah."

Scott's general view of the Old Testament prophets was shared by many who were not Evangelicals. For example, Charles Kingsley's argument that God still sends prophets to guide man is obviously based upon this conception of the prophet as forthspeaker rather than foreteller. According to Kingsley, a Broad Churchman, the Lord does not leave us unguarded when "the lying spirit comes and whispers to us . . . that we shall prosper in our wickedness . . . [but] sends His prophets to us, as He sent Micaiah [sic] to Ahab, to tell us that the wages of sin is death—to tell us that those who sow the wind shall reap the whirlwind—to set before us at every turn, that we may choose between them, and live or die according to our choice."[10] This view of the prophet as divine messenger, or one who speaks out on crucial issues, was recognized even by those without orthodox belief, thus suggesting how widely current it was in the last century. T. H. Huxley, certainly no believer, thus pointed out that "the term prophecy applies as much to outspeaking as foretelling; and, even in the restricted sense of 'divination,' it is obvious that the essence of the prophetic operation does not lie in its backward or forward relation to the course of time, but in the fact that it is the apprehension of that which lies out of the sphere of immediate knowledge; the seeing of which, to the natural sense of the seer, is invisible."[11]

[10]"Self-Destruction," *Village Sermons, and Town and Country Sermons* (London, Macmillan, 1886), p. 63.
[11]"On the Method of Zadig" (1880), *Science and Hebrew Tradition* (New

In addition, the Victorian sage adopts not only the general tone and stance of the Old Testament prophet but also the quadripartite pattern with which the prophet usually presents his message.[12] According to Scott, who presents the orthodox view of his subject, the prophets of the Old Testament first called attention to their audience's present grievous condition and often listed individual instances of suffering. Second, they pointed out that such suffering resulted directly from their listeners' neglecting—falling away from—God's law. Third, they promised further, indeed deepened, miseries if their listeners failed to return to the fold; and fourth, they completed the prophetic pattern by offering visions of bliss that their listeners would realize if they returned to the ways of God. Many of these visions took the form of predictions of divine vengeance upon the irreligious heathen, who having served as God's agent for punishing the wayward Israelites would in future serve as an informing example of punishing wrath. For example, the Book of Isaiah "opens with sharp rebukes of the people for their idolatry and iniquity, and denunciations of divine vengeance upon them; but intermixed with encouraging intimations of mercy, and predictions of Christ. Afterwards follow various prophecies of judgments about to be executed on several nations, as well as on Judah; through all of which the reader is led to expect future deliverances and glorious times to the church of God."[13]

York, D. Appleton, 1901), p. 6. Huxley agrees with A. F. Kirkpatrick, Regius Professor of Theology at Cambridge, who held in *The Doctrine of the Prophets* (London, Macmillan, 1892), pp. 13–14, that "the prophet was not merely, I might even say he was not chiefly, a predictor. He was not so much a foreteller as a forthteller. Insight not less that foresight was the gift of the seer. The precise original meaning of the Hebrew word for prophet is much disputed. But it does not in itself contain the idea of prediction. In usage it denotes one who is the spokesman or interpreter of God to men, one who is the medium through which divine revelations are conveyed, rather than one who is endowed with the power of foreknowledge, though this may be one of his gifts."

[12]For modern views of prophetic structure, see Claus Westermann, *Basic Forms of Prophetic Speech*, trans. Hugh Clayton White (Philadelphia, Westminster Press, 1967). Bernhard W. Anderson, *Understanding the Old Testament* (Englewood Cliffs, N.J., Prentice-Hall, 1957), summarizes the history and development of Old Testament prophecy.

[13]*A Commentary on the Holy Bible*, 3: 81.

This prophetic pattern of interpretation, attack upon the audience (or those in authority), warning, and visionary promise, provides the single most important influence of the Bible upon the writings of the original Victorian sages, for it gives rise to many, though not all, of the devices that make up this characteristically Victorian genre. Biblical prophecy—and contemporary understanding of biblical prophecy—also provide the ultimate source of the discontinuous, episodic structures found in this genre and perhaps also of the audience's willingness to accept them. Theories of biblical prophecy therefore seem to have had much the same effect upon notions of literary structure that theories of the sublime had upon notions of aesthetics: In the same way that the apparent disorder of sublimity allowed Augustan critics to compensate for the restrictions and omissions of neoclassical conceptions of beauty, biblical prophecy allowed them to find acceptable forms of literary organization outside the neoclassical canon. According to Campegius Vitringa's *Typus Doctrinae Propheticae* (1708), which appeared in John Gill's popular Bible commentary, prophecies often "admit of resumptions, repetitions of sayings, and retrograde leaps and skips, or scattered or detached pieces . . . which are inserted into the text, for the sake of illustrating this or that part of the prophecy. . . . To these may also be rightly referred the excursions and digressions, in which the prophets, whilst they really have before their eyes some object of more remote time, suddenly leave it, and by way of excursion turn themselves to men of their own time, or the next; that from the subject of their prophecy, they may admonish, exhort and convince them."[14] Vitringa might be describing *Past and Present*, *The Stones of Venice*, or works by twentieth-century sages.

In addition to Old Testament prophecy, two other biblical traditions have a major effect upon this literary form—New Testament apocalyptics and typological exegetics. Carlyle and Ruskin draw heavily upon typological exegesis in their characteristic

---

[14]Quoted by Leslie Tannenbaum, *Biblical Tradition in Blake's Early Prophecies: The Great Code of Art* (Princeton, Princeton University Press, 1982), pp. 30, 32–39.

works.[15] Nonetheless, their writing as sages derives far more importantly from late-eighteenth- and nineteenth-century attitudes toward Old Testament prophecy. Although scriptural typology accounts for both the sage's general attitude toward interpretation and the meaning of specific passages, Old Testament prophecy is directly responsible for the overall nature of this literary form as well as for many of its crucial characteristics, such as the sage's contentious attitude toward his audience, his alternation of satire and vision, and his use of discontinuous literary structure.[16]

Although twentieth-century sages tend not to employ the full prophetic structure that marks Victorian works in this form, they employ all the other devices of the sage. These include (1) a characteristic alternation of satire and positive, even visionary statement, that is frequently accompanied by (2) a parallel alternation of attacks upon the audience and attempts to reassure or inspire it; (3) a frequent concentration upon apparently trivial phenomena as the subject of interpretation; (4) an episodic or discontinuous literary structure that depends upon analogical rela-

---

[15]See George P. Landow, *Victorian Types, Victorian Shadows: Biblical Typology in Victorian Literature, Art, and Thought* (Boston, Routledge & Kegan Paul, 1980), pp. 110–18, 166–76. For a discussion of the influence of this form of scriptural interpretation upon American literature, see Ursula Brumm, *American Thought and Religious Typology*, trans. John Hoaglund (New Brunswick, Rutgers University Press, 1970), *Typology and Early American Literature*, ed. Sacvan Bercovitch (Amherst, University of Massachusetts Press, 1972), and Karl Keller, "Alephs, Zahirs, and the Triumph of Ambiguity: Typology in Nineteenth-Century American Literature," in *Literary Uses of Typology from the Middle Ages to the Present*, ed. Earl Miner (Princeton, Princeton University Press, 1977), pp. 274–314.

[16]The recent work of Mary W. Carpenter and Lawrence Poston on apocalyptics and nineteenth-century millenarianism also promises to shed much light upon this as well as other Victorian genres. Mary W. Carpenter, the first student of Victorian literature and thought to examine at all closely the many nineteenth-century interpretations of the Apocalypse, provides much essential background in "The Apocalypse of the Old Testament: *Daniel Deronda* and the Interpretation of Interpretation," *PMLA* 99 (1984): 56–71, and "The Structures of Time: George Eliot and the Apocalyptic Structure of History" (Brown University Ph.D. dissertation, 1983). See also Mary W. Carpenter and George P. Landow, "Ambiguous Revelations: The Apocalypse in Victorian Literature," in *The Apocalypse in English Renaissance Thought and Literature*, ed. C. A. Patrides and Joseph Wittreich (Manchester, University of Manchester Press, 1985;

tions for unity and coherence; (5) a reliance upon grotesque contemporary phenomena, such as the murder of children, or grotesque metaphor, parable, and analogy; (6) satiric and idiosyncratic definitions of key terms; (7) and an essential reliance upon *ethos*, or the appeal to credibility. The first five of these techniques obviously derive from the prophetic pattern, and the last two function to accommodate it to the situation in which the Victorian sage finds himself—to the situation, that is, in which he no longer speaks literally as the prophet of God.

Since Milton, Blake, and Wordsworth all draw upon the traditions of Old Testament prophecy and even occasionally present themselves as prophets, why do they not have a place in this study of the sage? Or, to point this question differently, why do I believe they do not write as sages in the sense that I define the term? The answer has little to do with the fact that they write in verse while those I consider sages write in prose. The answer lies instead in these poets' relations to their audiences, for although, as James H. Coombs has shown, Milton and Wordsworth shared many assumptions about themselves as poet-prophets, neither wrote with that particularly contentious, eccentric, opposing vantage point of both the Old Testament prophet and the Victorian sage.[17] Milton, of course, describes himself in *Paradise Lost* and elsewhere as an isolated prophet courageously presenting unwelcome truths, but in practice—the practice of justifying the ways of God to man—he writes as an epic poet and from the self-assured position of the epic poet. However much he dramatizes himself as a beleaguered prophet, Milton (like Wordsworth) writes as if his message is a central, rather than an eccentric, one, and he therefore does not employ the kind of rhetorical devices adopted by the sage. The case is similar with Blake, but

Ithaca, Cornell University Press, 1985), pp. 299–322. Lawrence Poston, "Millites and Millenarians: The Context of Carlyle's 'Signs of the Times,'" *Victorian Studies* 26 (1982–83): 381–406, is an important study of the influence of a single example of millenarianism upon Carlyle.

[17]James H. Coombs, "Wordsworth and Milton: Poet-Prophets" (Brown University Ph.D. dissertation, 1985), provides valuable comments on this subject of poetic prophecy and its tradition. See also William Kerrigan, *The Prophetic Milton* (Charlottesville, University Press of Virginia, 1974), and *Milton and the Line of Vision*, ed. Joseph Wittreich (San Marino, Huntington Library, 1979).

other factors also distinguish his writings from those of the sage. In the first place, his manner of publication, which greatly restricted the size of his audience, prevented him from having the kind of public encounter with an audience that characterizes the earlier sages. Second, there is the matter of his poetic obscurity, which also both restricts the size of his audience and prevents his producing the abrasive effect of the sage.

Ralph Waldo Emerson, a friend to both Carlyle and Thoreau, represents another interesting test case for this theory of genre since an examination of his works suggests some questions of central importance. First, in what ways does this major writer of nonfiction relate to the nineteenth-century sage and his modern heirs? Does my proposed definition of a genre accurately describe his works, or does he write a somewhat different kind of prose or even an essentially different one? Second, if Emerson's writings do not match some of the defining characteristics of the sage's genre, how does this result affect the value of such generic description? Furthermore, does this generic description prove useful when reading other, possibly related, genres?

Many of the sage's concerns and techniques certainly appear in Emerson's writing. He employs a discontinuous literary structure, argument by image and analogy, acts of definition, and visionary promises, and he also uses many techniques to transfer the audience's allegiance to him. Nonetheless, Emerson does not strike one as a sage but as a writer in the ancient wisdom tradition. Two factors or qualities distinguish him from Carlyle, Thoreau, and others who created the genre of the sage. In the first place, the more genial Emerson almost never attacks his audience directly. He avoids directly confronting readers with their faults and flaws, although not because he lacks the satirist's gifts. When I first began to look for identifying characteristics of a possible genre, I thought of those writers who contributed to it under the rubric of "sages and satirists"; that is, I thought of them as those who combined some of the characteristics of traditional wisdom literature with those of satire. One of my colleagues, a well-known authority on the American literary renaissance, asserted that Emerson did not fit my requirements for a practitioner of this putative genre, largely because he never wrote satire. In fact, as I discovered, Emerson frequently employs satire, both its gentle philosophical form and a more traditional pointed one. Emerson certainly matches the savagery of Thoreau and Ruskin when he satirizes the state of English religion:

> The religion of England is part of good-breeding. When you see on the continent the well-dressed Englishman come into his ambassador's chapel, and put his face for silent prayer into his smooth-brushed hat, one cannot help feeling how much national pride prays with him, and the religion of a gentleman. So far is he from attaching any meaning to the words, that he believes himself to have done almost the generous thing, and that it is very condescending in him to pray to God.... Their religion is a quotation; their church is a doll; and any examination is interdicted with screams of terror. In good company you expect them to laugh at the fanaticism of the vulgar; but they do not: they are the vulgar.... The Anglican church is marked by the grace and good sense of its forms, by the manly grace of its clergy. The gospel it preaches, is, "By taste are ye saved." ... It is not in ordinary a persecuting church; it is not inquisitorial, not even inquisitive, is perfectly well-bred, and can shut its eyes on all proper occasions. ("Religion," *English Traits*, 886–88)

The closing sentences of this passage have much in common with attacks upon religious hypocrisy made by Ruskin and Thoreau, but a difference immediately strikes one: Emerson attacks the English, who are foreigners, outsiders, whereas Thoreau and Ruskin attack their fellow citizens.

The second chief difference that divides Emerson from his friend Carlyle and other sages lies in the fact that, unlike them, he avoids the particular and almost never interprets specific contemporary phenomena. One distinguishing feature of the sage is his ability to unpack meaning after meaning from apparently trivial facts and events, and his characteristic manner of proceeding endows such minutiae with value. Both this manner of proceeding and the attitudes toward reality that make it possible derive largely from the Puritan (or Evangelical) tradition. Specifically, they derive from typological interpretations of the Scriptures which emphasize that both Old Testament history and its

31

fulfillment, both Moses and Christ, have real historical existence.[18] The first- and second-generation sages all developed within the context of such biblical interpretation, and although none of them ended their careers with anything like orthodox Christian belief, they all retained habits of mind derived from early-nineteenth-century Protestantism. Emerson, in contrast, developed within a New England Unitarianism that denied the importance of both scriptural history and the literal truth of the Bible. Lawrence Buell's fine study of the influence of Unitarian thought upon the American Transcendentalists points to the importance of its "figurative approach to truth. The free and creative use the Unitarians made of scripture and doctrine was a significant legacy to Transcendentalist style as well as thought. Their approach to the Bible was a near anticipation of the Emersonian habit of interpreting its supernatural elements metaphorically."[19] Unitarian rhetoric anticipates qualities of Transcendentalist prose that distinguish it from that of the sage, such as "the figurative approach to doctrine and (occasionally) language," which, argues Buell, betrays an "impulse to go beyond truth unadorned to celebrate the beauty of truth, an impulse which tends to accelerate as the subject gets more secular, the theological content gets more tenuous, and the writer concentrates more on the appearances or manifestations of his principle than the articulation of the principle itself" (134). The Unitarian tradition, however, does not diverge entirely from the more orthodox Protestant one upon which the sages draw, and the two traditions share many of the same attitudes toward oratory and style. Characteristics that Unitarian rhetoric, Transcendentalist prose, and Emerson's own writings do share with the work of Carlyle and other writers in this genre thus include what Buell describes as typical Unitarian "multiplicity of demonstration, often verging on catalogue rhetoric" and an "intermittent use of rhapsodic as

[18]See Landow, *Victorian Types, Victorian Shadows*, pp. 51–63.

[19]*Literary Transcendentalism: Style and Vision in the American Renaissance* (Ithaca, Cornell University Press, 1973), p. 114. Hereafter cited in text. Buell's excellent discussion of the nineteenth-century American sermon, particularly in its Unitarian form, demonstrates how very different were the American and British milieus at this time. See in particular pp. 105–10.

opposed to logical ordering" (134). Defining such literary techniques and both the literary and nonliterary traditions from which they derive helps us read individual works more richly and perceptively, and such an approach also suggests the complex interrelations between individual works, the genres in which they participate, and the traditions that they compose.

The fact that the theory of the sage does not embrace Emerson's writings implies little about its applicability and usefulness since it does not claim to describe all nineteenth- and twentieth-century nonfiction but only a single major strain or form. In fact, as long as it accurately describes a fair number of major works, and I believe it does, the theory proves useful because it can show us how to read and react to them. For this reason, defining the genre created by the Victorian and modern sage has value for understanding other forms of nonfiction as well. Because an approach by means of genre focuses attention upon particular literary techniques, it also helps us better appreciate those devices when they appear in other forms and at the same time it leads us to look more carefully at the way other forms employ alternative, or even diametrically opposed, techniques.

These considerations lead directly to similar ones specifically involving the twentieth-century sages, many of whom do not match every single part of my genre description. We have already seen that the prehistory or antecedents of the sage include the sermon tradition, Old Testament prophecy, and the interpretative tradition associated with both Testaments, and the genre also draws upon satire, both classical and neoclassical, and British and German romantic poetry as well. The formal type tentatively emerges first in Thomas Carlyle's "Signs of the Times" (1829) and then appears fully formed in *Chartism* (1839), *Past and Present* (1843), and *Latter-Day Pamphlets* (1850). Writings of the sage that obviously imitate Carlyle's works in this genre include many of the major landmarks of Victorian nonfiction, such as Ruskin's five volumes of *Modern Painters* (1843–60), *The Stones of Venice* (1851–53), *Unto This Last* (1860), and his later political writings; Henry David Thoreau's "Life Without Principle" (1854), "Slavery in Massachusetts" (1854), "A Plea for Captain John Brown" (1859) and his other antislavery papers; and Matthew Arnold's *Culture and Anarchy* (1869) and *Friendship's Garland* (1871). Twentieth-century works that exemplify this developed phase of sage-writing include D. H. Lawrence's *Twilight in Italy* (1916), *Sea and Sardinia* (1921), *Etruscan Places* (1932), and *The Fantasia of the Unconscious* (1923); Norman Mailer's *Armies of the Night* (1968), *Miami and the Siege of Chicago* (1968), and *Of a Fire on the Moon* (1971); and Joan Didion's *Slouching towards Bethlehem* (1968) and *The White Album* (1979).

Twentieth-century practitioners of this mode produce works that differ in some significant ways from those of their predecessors despite major continuities of theme and technique. They still concentrate upon the same basic subjects, which include concerns to define the human, to restore the powers of language, to warn against the danger to man of technology (or mechanism), to examine the possibility of achieving heroism or the human ideal in a modern age, and above all, to read the Signs of the Times to save the audience from potential disaster. Furthermore, the same emphasis upon interpretation, definition, and prophetic warning appears in twentieth-century instances of the genre. Two obvious differences, however, distinguish Victorian from modern writings of the sage. First, because Carlyle, Thoreau, Ruskin, and Arnold shared with their audience a thorough knowledge of the Bible and the interpretative traditions by which it was most commonly understood, they could salt their works with complex, often witty, allusions to them. Such scriptural allusion, which conveniently authenticated the sage's claims to high seriousness, also created a sense of community between the sage and his audience, even when he no longer held to any orthodox Christian belief. In fact, the use of such methods not only borrowed some of the preacher's prestige and authority but also tended to reassure the sage's audience by disguising how unorthodox some of his ideas might be. Now that writers and a major part of their audience barely know the Bible at all, these techniques of sophisticated allusion have fallen by the way.

Second, modern practitioners of the form tend to place much more emphasis upon creating credibility by informing the reader about their weaknesses and shortcomings. Although Victorian sages frequently open lectures, essays, or books with a pose of humility, they quickly assert their superiority over the audience. Modern sages, in contrast, may inform their readers more specifically about personal weakness and also enter into intimate details of health and behavior. Part of this different approach and tone arises from the way Victorian and modern attitudes toward knowledge diverge. Although the Victorian sages admit that they live in an age of transition and shaken belief, they nonetheless claim to have a clear view of the issues, and this confidence assists their enterprise, which involves first winning a hearing from their audience and then gaining its credence. Although both Victorian and modern authors who write in this mode face audiences equally skeptical about their controversial interpretations, the modern audience is far more skeptical about the possibility of attaining any true knowledge at all, and therefore initial assertions of confidence will alienate it. Modern sages therefore necessarily present themselves as groping toward the truth.

Thus far we have considered only writings of the sage that exhibit a full repertoire of characteristic literary devices, but a considerable amount of interesting twentieth-century nonfiction turns out to use many, though not all, of the same devices. Therefore, after setting forth the range of devices that characterize the writings of the sage, I shall briefly discuss contemporary work that employs some of them. The writings of Germaine Greer, Tom Wolfe, John McPhee, Hunter Thompson, and many of the New Journalists exemplify work that benefits from discussion within the context provided by my notion of this genre. Such an approach, I must emphasize, is intended to permit us to read these and other works of nonfiction more perceptively and more enjoyably and not to create a means of separating the sage's wheat from the chaff of other associated forms.

Since the preceding discussion of sage-writing might seem to employ a potentially puzzling mixture of historical and ahistorical approaches, let us observe in what ways it follows historical method and in what ways, or on what occasions, it does not. To begin with, what does one mean by historical approaches to the

35

study of literary genre? To this query I respond that there are at least five ways of locating the individual genre in history, the first and most basic of which takes the form of making a descriptive definition. Since the conception of sage-writing I have advanced concerns already existing works rather than an ideal exemplar—what Carlyle and Thoreau wrote rather than a prescriptive formula for the genre—it is historical, indeed inevitably and essentially so. The second historical approach to genre that I have employed investigates its sources and origin, a project the previous pages have carried out by pointing to the derivation of the sage's techniques from sermons, satire, and Scripture. A third approach, which this study does not much employ, examines the specific situation that occasioned an individual work, and a fourth investigates the more general reason such works appear in a particular society and at a particular time.[20] The fifth historical approach, which this work does not follow, studies a genre's transmission from work to work and author to author, concentrating on the influence of one author upon another.

Elegant Jeremiahs relies primarily upon the first two of these approaches, the first because it is fundamental to all others and the second because it offers a clear, convenient means of carrying out the first. Strictly speaking, however, genre definition does not require explanations as to how genres arise or how they are transmitted between individual works and writers. The assertion that one can apply generic description to works written in different times and places at first glance might appear ahistorical, but it is not and only appears to be so because this notion of sage-writing is itself somewhat novel. Writers on lyric poetry and the novel rarely feel obliged to trace the exact heritage of specific techniques or themes, just because they assume the existence of genre and the fact of generic transmission.[21] This book pur-

[20]The obvious explanation why sage-writing appears in both Victorian and modern times is that in ages during which the author seems removed from a central position of influence, he or she finds attractive sets of techniques (genres) developed earlier in similar historical situations. The question next arises whether these genres are handed down or re-created anew, whether matters of influence or confluence.

[21]Transferring critical emphasis from the influence of one work (or author) upon another to the notion of a group of works encourages one to appreciate

posely does not examine the influence of Victorians upon each other and of Victorians upon moderns. It makes little attempt, for example, to prove that Carlyle influenced Thoreau or that Didion and Mailer consciously drew upon their nineteenth-century predecessors, and it does not do so for several reasons.[22] A full study of influences and confluences, such as David DeLaura's *Hebrew and Hellene in Victorian England,* is more than double the size of this work. But length is not the only or chief argument against trying *in this book* to map influences and interrelations: Doing so distracts from the main issue and can disguise weaknesses in theory. If my conception of sage-writing provides a useful way into the writings under consideration, some of which are not usually considered together, then it works, whereas if it does not, then assertions of influence and source studies become meaningless as a means of proof.

In fact, if this description of the genre created by the sage offers a useful approach to both nineteenth- and twentieth-century writings—to, say, certain works of Carlyle and Mailer—then it has produced important results whether or not one can demon-

---

complex literary relationships. Thus, when Ernst Curtius set forth his idea of rhetorical *topoi* and metaphorics in *European Literature and the Latin Middle Ages* (1948), trans. Willard R. Trask (New York, Pantheon, 1953), he created opportunities for more sophisticated conceptions of source and influence. Noticing that both Catullus and Cassian described their works as boats setting out on a perilous voyage, those who employ older methods might claim to have discovered direct influence (pp. 128–29). By pointing out the nature and function of such rhetorical commonplaces, Curtius revealed that cases like that of Cassian and Dante involving textual resemblance are better understood in terms of a tradition from which both authors have drawn. One may add that Curtius thus shows that literary relations are better described in terms of webs or networks of relationships than as single lines of force. For a discussion of a related approach to more recent literature, see George P. Landow, *Images of Crisis: Literary Iconology, 1750 to the Present* (Boston and London, Routledge & Kegan Paul, 1982).

[22]The materials from which to construct a picture of Victorian influence and confluence are of course readily available. One can easily determine at least the broader parameters of the Carlyle-Ruskin relationship now that we have *The Correspondence of Thomas Carlyle and John Ruskin,* ed. George Allen Cate (Stanford, Stanford University Press, 1982), and Thoreau offers abundant evidence of his knowledge of Carlyle in "Thomas Carlyle and His Works" (1847), in *Early Essays and Miscellanies,* ed. Joseph J. Moldenhauer, Edwin Moser, and Al-

strate specific lines of influence and inspiration. I would claim that a situation in which one could not find any evidence of such influence of Victorian upon modern authors would prove particularly interesting for an examination of this genre, since it would suggest that specific social, political, and literary situations generate specific kinds of writing—that similar contexts prompt the weaving of similar texts. Although I do not believe that such a situation obtains here, the origins of both ancient Greek and medieval European drama in religious ritual show that such a possibility is not as outlandish as it might at first seem.

Before continuing this examination of the sage's writings, I want to make clear another aspect of the approach adopted in the following pages. To describe the genre of the sage, I have chosen to concentrate upon examining those techniques that, when taken together, constitute this literary form. I have therefore not organized the individual chapters in this book around themes, authors, or individual works.[23] Instead, each of the following chapters examines a single technique or group of closely related techniques and provides examples of them. Each chapter begins with instances drawn from the writings of the Victorian sages—and I include the American Thoreau under this rubric—and then offers additional ones taken from twentieth-century authors, particularly when these more recent authors modify or give their own coloring to the sage's techniques. With the exception of the first chapter, which concerns itself largely with the prophetic pattern that only the Victorian sages employ ex-

---

exander C. Kern (Princeton, Princeton University Press, 1975), pp. 219–67. For discussions of the influence of Carlyle and Ruskin upon Lawrence, see the relevant chapters in *D. H. Lawrence and Tradition*, ed. Jeffrey Meyers (London, Athlone Press, 1985). There is far less evidence about more recent authors' knowledge of Carlyle, Ruskin, and Thoreau or their indebtedness to them, but Didion explicitly refers to Ruskin, and Wolfe follows Ruskinian method in his own works on art and architecture. See chapter 2, note 16, below.

[23] I have made a preliminary attempt at mapping out the genre in terms of a single work by Ruskin in "Ruskin as Victorian Sage: The Example of 'Traffic,'" in *New Approaches to Ruskin*, ed. Robert Hewison (London, Routledge & Kegan Paul, 1981), pp. 89–110. For presentation of his entire career in these terms, see George P. Landow, *Ruskin*, Past Masters (Oxford, Oxford University Press, 1985).

plicitly, each devotes approximately equal space to nineteenth-
and twentieth-century examples.

Although such an attempt to define the genre created by the
writings of the sages ultimately aids in interpreting individual
works (since genre rules and genre recognition determine our
rules of interpretation), the following pages do not concern
themselves largely with interpreting entire works or even long
passages from them. The passages cited serve chiefly as a means
of setting forth a useful taxonomy of the techniques that define
and limit this literary form. My approach will be to examine passages that exemplify one or more techniques of the sage in order
to define those techniques, chart their contributions to the
genre, and indicate their intended effects upon the audience. In
making such descriptive analyses and analytical descriptions, one
quickly encounters instances of what I take to be a central axiom
of literary form, one that applies with equal force to the individual work and to its interpretation—all facts in a work, all facets
of a work, are multidetermined, and therefore no one
explanation of any literary phenomenon suffices. In terms of this
attempt to make an accurate description of the congeries of techniques that make up the genre of the sage, this axiom of multi-
determinateness suggests what indeed turns out to be the case;
namely, that individual techniques simultaneously participate in
various regions of our taxonomy: Individual techniques, such as
the use of bravado interpretation or grotesque set pieces, frequently also function as a means of satire, defining language, or
both. Few individual passages provide examples of only one technique or of a technique used singly.

At the same time that the following chapters thus set out to
describe the individual techniques that together comprise the
writings of the sage, they also point to the roots of such techniques, and hence of the genre, in other often extraliterary
genres (or ones that readers today tend to consider extraliterary,
such as sermons, biblical commentaries, and the Bible itself). Although individual techniques rarely remain completely
unmodified when they appear in the writings of the sage, the
roots often appear quite easy to perceive, and this fact suggests
two important points. First, it is the combination of these

39

literary and rhetorical strategies that constitute this genre rather than any particular one of them; and second, each of these techniques has roots in another genre or genres. In other words, each technique provides a necessary and sufficient—but by no means unique—"cause" of this genre. For example, ethos, the appeal to credibility, provides what I take to be the one essential technique, one that is the result or effect of all the other techniques of the sage working in combination, but it is by no means unique to the writings of Carlyle and the other creators of this form, as indeed its very name, taken from the old manuals of rhetoric, indicates. Nonetheless, as we shall observe, ethos in the writings of the sage differs from that in other literary forms, if only because it becomes the major effect and not merely a subsidiary or contributing one.

As the reader will gather from the preceding descriptions of method, I do not intend this study of the sage to be encyclopedic, and I have omitted from discussion many obvious examples of Victorian and modern sage-writings. Similarly, although it is possible that works of writers outside the Anglo-American tradition, such as Friedrich Nietzsche, Miguel de Unamuno, and E. M. Cioran, have much in common with this genre, I have chosen to concentrate upon its English and American inventors and some major instances of twentieth-century practitioners of the form. By surveying the techniques that characterize this genre, I hope to clarify the implicit rules for reading it. If we can ascertain the proper way to read the writings of the sages—the way, that is, the works themselves indicate—we shall also attain to a better understanding of individual instances of the genre, its relation to other literary forms, and the history and development of nonfictional prose.

1

The Prophetic Pattern

Acts of Interpretation

Like the Old Testament prophet, the Victorian sage and his modern heirs begin their statements by announcing the crucial need to understand some unhappy fact or event in contemporary life. In *Chartism* the particular puzzling phenomenon Carlyle uses as his point of departure is the discontent of the working classes: "What means this bitter discontent of the Working Classes? . . . How inexpressibly useful were true insight into it; a genuine understanding by the upper classes of society what it is that the under classes intrinsically *mean*; a clear *interpretation* of the thought which at heart torments these wild inarticulate souls, struggling there, with inarticulate uproar, like dumb creatures in pain, unable to speak what is in them! Something they do *mean*; some true thing withal, in the centre of their confused hearts" (29.119, 122; italics added). Carlyle emphatically states the sage's two basic premises, the first of which is that the particular phenomenon to which he draws attention possesses significant meaning and is not simply a random occurrence. The second premise of the sage is that this uncovered meaning is important, even crucial to his audience's survival. Therefore the sage's first step, the one for which we obviously need him, is to reveal the presence of meanings by drawing the audience's attention to some phenomenon, such as working-class unrest, which demands comprehension.

In *Past and Present* the sage's opening gambit draws the reader's attention to "one of the most ominous, and withal one of the strangest" phenomena:

> England is full of wealth, of multifarious produce, supply for human want in every kind; yet England is dying of inanition. With unabated bounty the land of England blooms and grows; waving with yellow harvest; thick-studded with workshops, industrial implements, with fifteen millions of workers, understood to be the strongest, the cunningest and the willingest our Earth ever had; these men are here; the work they have done, the fruit they have realised is here, abundant, exuberant on every hand of us: and behold, some baleful fiat as of Enchantment has gone forth, saying, "Touch it not, ye workers, ye master-workers, ye master-idlers; none of you can touch it, no man of you shall be the better for it; this is enchanted fruit!" (10.1)

In several ways this passage serves as a fitting paradigm of the sage's first move or opening technique, because in it Carlyle simultaneously proclaims his subject, indicates its importance to his audience, and suggests, in part by the power of his rhetoric, a confidence in his ability to answer the questions he has raised by pointing to the subject in the first place. Furthermore, lending his voice to that "baleful fiat"—to whatever has caused such human want in the midst of such abundance—Carlyle makes explicit one of the sage's chief techniques: he acts as a ventriloquist, providing an eloquent voice for inanimate phenomena and inarticulate masses. The sage proceeds by turning "dumb facts" into speaking voices.

In addition, Carlyle, who frequently calls the reader's attention to this first crucial stage in his enterprise, also implies that he serves as a second Daniel, interpreting writing on the wall, and as a second (though pre-Freudian) Oedipus. These metaphors for the sage's interpretations, which he draws from classical mythology and the Old Testament, emphasize the essential importance to the community of his acts of interpretation. *Chartism*, for instance, presents the longed-for interpreter of contemporary political phenomena as Oedipus confronting the Sphinx when he asks: "What are the rights, what are the mights of the discontented Working Classes in England at this epoch? He were an Oedipus, and deliverer from sad social pestilence, who could resolve us fully!" (29.123). Oedipus, we recall, rid Thebes of the Sphinx by solving her riddle. "What walks on four feet in the morning, two at noon, and three in the evening?" she demanded, and the hero responded that the answer is man, who crawls upon all four limbs as a baby, walks erect as an adult, and totters about with the aid of a cane in the evening of life. Upon hearing Oedipus's solution to her riddle, the Sphinx, who had plagued Thebes, hurled herself to her death. The Greek hero thus saved a community by comprehending the nature of man. In essence every sage attempts to do the same, for no matter what his point of departure, no matter what phenomenon he interprets, he ends up trying to define some crucial aspect of the human.

In yet another Carlylean metaphor events appear as fire-letters or writing on the wall: "France is a pregnant example in all ways. Aristocracies that do not govern, Priesthoods that do not teach; the misery of that, and the misery of altering that,—are written in Belshazzar fire-letters on the history of France" (29.161–62).[1] Carlyle alludes, of course, to the Book of Daniel, in which the prophet comes forth to read the undecipherable letters of judgment that have appeared on the wall of Belshazzar's palace.[2] The fifth chapter of the Book of Daniel relates that on

[1] Then again the sage appears as an Understanding Eye, as society's organ of understanding the mysteriously encoded, for as he explains, "Events are written lessons, glaring in huge hieroglyphic picture-writing, that all may read and know them: the terror and horror they inspire is but the note of preparation for the truth they are to teach; a mere waste of terror if that not be learned" (29.155).

[2] In thus citing a nonbiblical event as a modern example of writing on the wall, Carlyle made the same use of this situation that Victorian preachers did. F. D. Maurice wrote, for example: "If the earthquake of Lisbon swept away hundreds and thousands, of whom we cannot pronounce that they were worse than we are,—at least we may hear in it a voice denouncing those same sins which brought death upon Korah and his company; the ambition and falsehood of

43

the night that Belshazzar made a feast for a thousand of his lords, there "came forth fingers of a man's hand, and wrote . . . upon the plaister of the wall of the king's palace" (5:5). When his astrologers and soothsayers cannot read the writing upon the wall, Belshazzar in desperation calls for Daniel, who reminds him that God had raised Nebuchadnezzar, his father, above other kings and then hurled him low when he became proud and arrogant. After telling the king that the same judgment has come to him, he interprets the meaning of the mysterious writing:

> And this *is* the writing that was written, MENE, MENE, TEKEL, UPHARSIN.
> This *is* the interpretation of the thing: MENE; God hath numbered thy kingdom, and finished it.
> TEKEL; Thou art weighed in the balances, and art found wanting.
> PERES; Thy kingdom is divided, and given to the Medes and the Persians. (5:25–28)

Daniel's reading of the divine sentence of course does not function as a warning to the king since Belshazzar has so sinned that he put himself beyond salvation. Daniel's prophetic interpretations, which verses 30 and 31 reveal to have been accurate, authenticate his stature as a prophet at the same time that they convey a generalizable divine warning: God punishes with terrible destruction all those who fall from his way. Furthermore, because nineteenth-century exegetes read the Book of Daniel as an Old Testament analogue to the Book of Revelation of St. John the Divine, they generally found that its situations had been divinely intended to prefigure those of their own time; and Carlyle, who had been trained as a minister, plays with such expectations.

Another, more common version of the sage's announcement of

---

priests leading to the unbelief, sensuality, godlessness of a people. It was a handwriting on the wall addressed to all Europe. The attempts of the seers and soothsayers of the age to decypher it, showed that they felt it to be so" ("The Rebellion of Korah," *The Patriarchs and Lawgivers of the Old Testament* [London, Macmillan, 1892], p. 214). Maurice next asserts that the French Revolution similarly served as handwriting on the wall.

for its creation. Third, says Ruskin, that miserable bit of fencing represents the dangerous work at the blast furnace required to produce the iron it contains (and he quotes a recent newspaper article about the particularly horrible deaths of two men burned to death by molten metal). Fourth, that pub fence represents "ill-taught students making bad designs" (18.388), so that this bit of contemporary work "from the beginning to the last fruits of it" represents all that is deadly and miserable in British society. Ruskin as sage thereupon inquires why this kind of work was done rather than that which would have been enlivening: "How did it come to pass that this work was done instead of the other; that the strength and life of the English operative were spent in defiling ground, instead of redeeming it, and in producing an entirely (in that place) valueless, piece of metal, which can neither be eaten nor breathed, instead of medicinal fresh air and pure water?" (18.388). Having begun by looking at the litter that has collected behind an ugly, if expensive iron railing, Ruskin reveals the many significant truths that metal barrier embodies, after which he shows its relation to contemporary political economy. The progression is as unexpected as Ruskin's initial choice of such humble materials for his subject; he and other sages take grave rhetorical risks when they work in this manner, but when Ruskin succeeds in thus revealing significance where no such significance seems possible, he authenticates his claims to extraordinary perception and extraordinary understanding.

In *The White Album* Joan Didion offers a twentieth-century example of interpreting Signs of the Times that is characteristic of recent versions or extensions of this genre because at the same time that it emphasizes the essentially arrogant act of interpretation, it humbly admits the author's difficulties in comprehending her subject. The title essay of Didion's *White Album* opens with this typically modern intonation of the sage's search for meaning, for while she reminds us that the urge to make sense of things, of our lives, and of what happens to us answers to an essential human need—to a need as basic as that for food and sleep—she also lets us know that she herself doubts whether such a project is even possible. Her admission of doubt, which serves to convince the reader that she is like him, paradoxically goes a long way to creating the effect of credibility because we know that she will retail no familiar saws, no used-up answers; we know too that she has experienced and survived those very doubts that made her enterprise necessary to us in the first place. If she fails to answer our need, well, at least she has tried honestly to find a solution (so we feel upon encountering such an open admission of weakness), and we therefore shall have, at the very minimum, a companion in our wanderings. But, if she has something to offer, we shall be all the more willing to take it seriously.

Didion begins her snapshot-history of the 1960s by emphasizing that in order to live we try to impose a fictional order upon the welter of fact and experience amid which we find ourselves: "We tell ourselves stories in order to live," she insists, and then she heaps up instances of things about which she has tried to tell herself stories in order to live:

> The princess is caged in the consulate. The man with the candy will lead the children into the sea. The naked woman on the ledge outside the window on the sixteenth floor is a victim of accidie, or the naked woman is an exhibitionist, and it would be "interesting" to know which. We tell ourselves that it makes some difference whether the naked woman is about to commit a mortal sin or is about to register a political protest or is about to be, the Aristophanic view, snatched back to the human condition by the fireman in priest's clothing just visible in the window behind her, the one smiling at the telephoto lens. We look for the sermon in the suicide, for the social or moral lesson in the murder of five.
> (*White Album*, 11)

Like Carlyle and Ruskin before her, Didion thrusts forward a grotesque assemblage of encountered fact, and, also like them, she reveals that she has come upon one of the Signs of the Times to which we must pay close attention. Like her predecessors, she also has chosen to force apparently trivial matters upon our attention, for however bizarre they may seem to us, none of the images she proffers at first seem to bear any major significance. Would-be suicides, protestors, or what-have-we are all alas so common that we hardly pause over them any more. Of course, Didion's proffered album contains pictures, snapshots, which turn

47

out to be secondhand. The disguised fireman, for example, has been captured from that enigmatic event not by Didion's memory but by a newspaper photograph of it; and that secondhandness, like the fact that her memory (our memory) has been stored with images made by others preserved with the aid of modern technology, is itself a Sign of the Times—indeed, perhaps one of the most significant.

These events and the photographic images that record them have intruded themselves upon Didion's consciousness, and now, in her role as sage, she makes them intrude upon ours. For having tried them upon her own pulse and in the chambers of her own mind, she knows that they are significant, that they *are* Signs of the Times, and that to survive these times we must read them. We must interpret, and we must interpret correctly. According to her, writers exist to present connections between things and events, and she therefore has a double advantage over us—her career as writer has forced upon her the crucial recognition that the writer of fiction engages not in just one among many human activities but in the primal one that defines the human and also enables us to survive.

In the manner of the modern sage, she also admits doubt about both her own enterprise and her own ability to carry it out successfully. According to her, "We look for the sermon in the suicide, for the social or moral lesson in the murder of five." We must make them mean something. Therefore, "we interpret what we see, select the most workable of the multiple choices. We live entirely, especially if we are writers, by the imposition of a narrative line upon disparate images, by the 'ideas' with which we have learned to freeze the shifting phantasmagoria which is our actual experience" (*White Album*, 11). Thus far we have encountered a good old-fashioned generalization, a *sententia* such as Samuel Johnson might have advanced for our improvement, after which we have found ourselves amid a welter of puzzling images and have been told that we must understand them in order to live. At this point, Didion introduces the element of doubt, and in so doing she answers our curiosity about "why these images?" For after instructing us that we—and writers, in particular—live by imposing stories, order, upon that "shifting phantasmagoria

48

which is our actual experience," she reveals that her album captures the crucial fact about the 1960s in America: belief, the paradigmatic narrative that held society together, had disappeared.

In contrast to Didion's almost despairing presentation of the need to make such acts of interpretation, John McPhee never explicitly announces their problematic nature. McPhee, one of the most classical or Johnsonian of those twentieth-century practitioners of this genre, earns his position in this study of secular prophets by his resolute intention to interpret those contemporary phenomena that he finds to be clues to the heart and mind of his society. This superb reader of the Signs of the Times, who frequently invokes the Carlylean contrast of past and present, rarely emphasizes the grotesque elements of his symbolical materials even when they might seem to demand such emphasis. For example, *The Crofter and the Laird* opens and closes with obviously grotesque matters involving murders, bizarre loyalties, and equally bizarre betrayals of others. These tales of the McPhee clan's past serve to frame the balanced view of the modern tale that provides the subject of most of the book, but by placing them outside the main action, as it were, McPhee manages rather nicely to prevent them from obtruding upon a view of reality they might disturb and even disprove. Such grotesqueries provide interesting, entertaining reading, but they do not, as similar facts would in Carlyle or Mailer, appear particularly relevant to the present. Unlike many of his predecessors, McPhee does not transform grotesques into what Ruskin termed symbolical grotesques, and he does not do so because his basic method necessarily must defuse such materials to prevent them from obtruding upon his main themes. This avoidance of the grotesque—or rather this commitment to making his audience perceive that even the most seemingly grotesque phenomena have relevance to their lives—sharply contrasts him to those other sages, including Carlyle, Thoreau, Ruskin, Lawrence, and Mailer, who emphasize the grotesque nature of so many Signs of the Times precisely because they wish to emphasize how badly their contemporaries have fallen away from the true path. McPhee, one suspects, does not emphasize the obviously grotesque nature of some of the phenomena he cites for the same reason that he explicitly adopts a balanced structure in *The Crofter and the Laird, Coming into the Country,* and *Levels of the Game*: Grotesqueness is a product and sign of unbalance, and McPhee desires to present a balanced view, a view that simultaneously communicates an intellectual interpretation and a moral judgment (though in fact this moral judgment usually takes the form of spelling out the rights and wrongs of opposing sides). McPhee thus resembles Samuel Johnson more than any of the other. sages, even Arnold; but whereas Johnson used balanced periods in individual sentences and balanced paragraphs, McPhee's classicism, if I may term it that, appears in his judicially arranged major arguments. In other words, he most frequently begins a book by presenting one side of a case—he does appear to conceive them as cases—and follows this first view by one that opposes it.

Two things demand remark about his method. First, he does not generally follow his argument and counterargument with a conclusion, for he does not seem interested in, or apparently feel himself capable of, a synthesis. Indeed, the purpose of his method, which here appears very Arnoldian, seems to lie precisely in this final balance and tension; like that Victorian sage, McPhee holds up as an ideal the critical, inquiring mind that can examine both sides of a controversial question, thereby doing self and society a major service. It is not clear—just as it is not clear in Arnold—if such presentation of opposing views (often the politically liberal and the politically conservative) arises more from a pure commitment to the ideal of balance or merely from the journalist's inability to take sides.

Second, his method has as an unspoken assumption the notion that only two views exist, or that all possible views of a subject can be justly and accurately separated into two opposing positions. For all its obvious judiciousness and its equally obvious rhetorical advantages for McPhee, this means of presenting his subjects fits them into a mold as firmly as does the prose of Johnson or Macaulay, leaving no room for phenomena that have more than two rival interpretations.

Opposing the Audience

The second component of those strategies that constitute the prophetic pattern takes the form of directly opposing the audience, often by making it the object of explicit attack. As Thoreau, one of the most aggressive of sages, points out, people do not like to hear hard truth, but telling it to them is the sage's duty and prerogative: "All simple and necessary speech between men is sweet; but it takes calamity, it takes death or great good fortune commonly to bring them together. We are sages and proud to speak when we are the bearers of great news, even though it be hard; to tell a man of the welfare of his kindred in foreign parts, or even that his house is on fire, is a great good fortune, and seems to relate us to him by a worthier tie" ("Reform and the Reformers," 189).[3] The stance of the Old Testament prophet and the Victorian sage, however, involves more than announcing something important. One can join with his fellows when he conveys good news or bad, and telling someone that his house is on fire requires little more than a loud voice, but when one announces to his contemporaries that they unknowingly stand in burning houses and that their ignorance or evil kindled the flames, a particular posture becomes necessary. Thus, in Jeremiah 5:25 the inspired prophet announces to the Israelites: "Your iniquities have turned away these things, and your sins have withholden good things from you." Like the Old Testament prophet, therefore, the Victorian sage positions himself in conscious opposition to his audience or entire society. Even Emerson, who rarely writes as a sage, draws several times upon his knowledge of the prophetic tradition to describe aspects of the sage's method or ideas associated with it. In "The Young American" he urges upon his audience the "need of a withdrawal from the crowd, and a resort to the fountain of right, by the

---

[3]Thoreau, in fact, foreshadows modern biblical scholars, who trace the notion of the prophet to the Hebrew idea of precisely such a messenger and bringer of news. See James F. Ross, "The Prophet as Yahweh's Messenger," in *Israel's Prophetic Heritage: Essays in Honor of James Muilenburg*, ed. Bernhard W. Anderson and Walter Harrelson (New York, Harper, 1962), pp. 98–107, and Claus Westermann, *Basic Forms of Prophetic Speech* (Philadelphia, Westminster Press, 1967), pp. 98–128.

brave. The timidity of our public opinion, is our disease, or, shall I say, the publicness of opinion, the absence of private opinion. Good-nature is plentiful, but we want justice, with heart of steel, to fight down the proud" (227). The center of such a belief that one must inevitably stand apart from the mass of men to speak the truth derives ultimately, I suspect, from the more radical portions of Puritan and evangelical Protestantism. In its later, dechristianized form it appears as an Emersonian romantic individualism that assumes "the private mind has the access to the totality of goodness and truth, that it may be a balance to a corrupt society; and to stand for the private verdict against popular clamor, is the office of the noble" ("The Young American," 227).[4] The essentially Protestant roots of such Emersonian individualism appear in his assertion that "to believe in your own thought, to believe that what is true for you in your private heart is true for all men,—that is genius" ("Self-Reliance," 259).

Thoreau, who openly opposes and even attacks his audience in his antislavery writings, explains: "If . . . we find a certain Few standing aloof from the multitude—not allowing themselves to be carried along by the current of Popular feeling, we may fairly conclude that they have good reason for so doing—that they have looked farther into the subject than others," and he argues for his assumption that individuals tend to be superior to the masses of their fellows with the following analogy: "Those in the stream are not aware of the cataract at hand, but those on the bank have it in full view. Whose is the wisest and safest course?"[5]

Thoreau opens "Walking" by taking precisely such a stance, for he announces: "I wish to speak a word for Nature, for absolute freedom and wildness" and to consider man as "part and parcel of Nature, rather than a member of society." He emphasizes that he

[4]See M. H. Abrams, *Natural Supernaturalism: Tradition and Revolution in Romantic Literature* (New York, Norton, 1971), for the classic statement of ways in which romanticism transfers—and transmutes—elements of traditional Christianity.

[5]"Popular Feeling," *Early Essays and Miscellanies*, ed. Joseph J. Moldenhauer, Edwin Moser, and Alexander C. Kern (Princeton, Princeton University Press, 1975), p. 24.

wishes to make "an extreme statement," an emphatic one, "for there are enough champions of civilization: the minister and the school committee and every one of you will take care of that" (194). After announcing his theme in a relatively neutral tone, Thoreau abruptly becomes hostile and attacks his audience. Although he has immediately revealed that he would oppose the view of man as entirely a social being, he unexpectedly shows both that he himself stands apart from society and that he perceives its members as enemies.

As we see from Thoreau's example, one of the simplest and yet most powerful means by which the sage can distance himself from his audience is to use the second-person pronoun.[6] Such direct attack upon the audience is exemplified in Arnold's "My Countrymen," the opening chapter of *Friendship's Garland*: "*You* seem to think that *you* have only got to get on the back of *your* horse Freedom, or *your* horse Industry, and ride away as hard as *you* can, to be sure of coming to the right destination. If *your* newspapers can say what they like, *you* think *you* are sure of being well advised. That comes of *your* inaptitude for ideas, and aptitude for clap-trap" (5.22; italics added). In the succeeding chapters of *Friendship's Garland*, which purport to be letters to Arnold from Arminius, Baron von Thunder-ten-Tronckh, he adopts a manner more characteristic of the eighteenth-century satirist than of the Victorian sage since the harsh satire and pointed criticism supposedly come from an outsider. In the opening chapter, in contrast, such direct criticism comes explicitly from the writer himself, and the tone therefore resembles that found in the Vic-

---

[6]In "Reform and Reformers," Thoreau makes clear that an unwillingness to set oneself apart from others when necessary, say when one must save them from themselves by warning them of impending disaster, marks conservatives, who "naturally herd together for mutual protection" and naturally employ the first-person-plural pronoun: "They say *We* and *Our*, as if they had never been assured of an individual existence. *Our* Indian policy; *our* coast defences, *our* national character. They are what are called public men, fashionable men, ambitious men, chaplains of the army or navy; men of property, standing and respectability, for the most part, and in all cases created by society. Sometimes even they are embarked in 'Great Causes' which have been stranded on the shores of society in a previous age, carrying them through with a kind of reflected and traditionary nobleness" (181).

torian sermon or Old Testament prophecy more than in Swift or Pope.

Most writings of the nineteenth-century sages do not, however, employ the second-person so simply. Instead, they move back and forth between allying themselves with their audience and pulling away to attack it by shifting between *you* and *we*. Ruskin follows this manner of proceeding learned from Daniel, Jeremiah, Isaiah, and other Hebrew prophets. Like them he adroitly positions himself in relation to his audience. Only rarely in "Traffic"—for example, when he mentions that worship of the golden idols of Mammon is forbidden to "us"—does Ruskin place himself in the same position as his listeners. Only then does he permit them to take him as a man like them. On the other hand, gestures of opposition, rhetorical strategies that place him at a distance from his listeners, occur frequently in the course of his attack upon his audience and what he terms "this idol of yours" (18.457). Such risky rhetorical strategies both set this genre off from most other literary forms and inevitably require special techniques to avoid alienating the sage's intended audience. In other words the crucial difficulty in thus positioning the prophetic voice outside and above the society of the sage's intended listeners is that he must find a way to be superior to them, and to convince them that he is superior to them, without alienating them. Or, to state this fundamental problem in slightly different terms: the audience is willing to pay attention only to someone extraordinary and set apart from the majority of men, but any claim that one possesses special insight threatens to drive it away.

This characteristic positioning of himself as sage in relation to his listeners appears earlier in "Traffic" when Ruskin first instructs them that England will inevitably pass away and then, moving to solace his listeners, reassures them that they have such a dilemma only because they have been deluded by those Others, by the false prophets of *laissez-faire* capitalist economics. Ruskin opens this attack by forcing his listeners to realize that worshiping material success inevitably impoverishes a large portion of English society, after which he anticipates his audience's objections, openly admitting its hostility to him and his revelation: "You will tell me I need not preach against these things, for I cannot mend them. No, good friends, I cannot; but you can, and you will; or something else can and will. Even good things have no abiding power—and shall these evil things persist in victorious evil?" (18.455). Arguing that all history shows that change must come to men and societies, Ruskin adds that "it is ours to determine whether change of growth, or change of death" (18.455). Having briefly joined with his listeners when telling them that they can choose their own destinies, he immediately draws apart from them as, again striking the prophet's stance, he places contemporary phenomena in the context of eternity. "Shall the Parthenon," he asks, "be in the ruins on its rock, and Bolton Priory in its meadow, but these mills of yours be the consummation of the buildings of the earth, and their wheels as the wheels of eternity?" (18.455).

Having first complimented his listeners when he joined with them in the promise that they could choose their own fates, he withdraws from them to place the Signs of the Times within the context of ancient history and eternity. Ruskin then again draws close to his audience by partially absolving it for the present condition of England when he admits that his listeners have not wished to harm others: "I know that none of the wrong is done with deliberate purpose. I know, on the contrary, that you wish your workmen well; that you do much for them, and that you desire to do more for them, if you saw your way to such benevolence safely." Continuing to mix absolution and blame, he adds that he realizes that "even all this wrong and misery are brought about by a warped sense of duty." Then, after having partially absolved his listeners from blame for their treatment of British workers, Ruskin adopts the first-person-plural pronoun to join momentarily with his audience when he claims that "all our hearts have been betrayed by the plausible impiety of the modern economist, telling us that 'To do the best for ourselves, is finally to do the best for others'. Friends, our great Master said not so; and most absolutely we shall find this world is not made so" (18.455–56). Exchanging the second- for the first-person pronoun, Ruskin tries to loosen his audience's allegiance to utilitarian economics, for one way that the sage gains the assent of his

55

listeners is to compliment them or promise them hope after having revealed their perilous condition.

In "A Plea for Captain John Brown," Thoreau follows a very similar strategy in defending the great abolitionist.[7] He begins one movement or section of the "Plea" gently enough, aligning himself with his listeners and readers when he tells them, "Our foes are in our midst and all about us." Claiming that hardly a house "but is divided against itself," Thoreau finds the cause, the foe, in "the all but universal woodenness of both head and heart ... which is the effect of our vice" and which breeds "fear, supersitition, bigotry, persecution, and slavery of all kinds." Like Ruskin, Thoreau finds the root of the problem in a "worship of idols." Brown, he argues, was an exception, a true believer, "for he did not set up even a political graven image between him and his God." Having gently broached the topic of his audience's political, moral, and spiritual corruption, he then intensifies the charges by making them specific, after which he sets Brown apart from his audience. At this point Thoreau begins a new paragraph that violently attacks contemporary churches—and his audience as well. Brown set up no idols between himself and God; the churches, which betray Christ, do: "A church that can never have done with excommunicating Christ while it exists! Away with your broad and flat churches, and your narrow and tall churches! Take a step forward, and invent a new style of outhouses. Invent a salt that will save you, and defend our nostrils" (120). Thoreau's Swiftian analogy between his satiric target and excrement, like his impatient parody of high-, low-, and broad-church parties, climaxes in his use of *you* and *your*, since these

---

[7]Robert C. Albrecht, "Thoreau and His Audience: 'A Plea for Captain John Brown,'" *American Literature* 32 (1960–61): 393–402, makes some useful brief observations on Thoreau's use of pronouns and implied familiarity with his audience. Discussions of the historical setting to the "Plea" and the role of Brown in Thoreau's thought appear in Herbert L. Carson, "The Eccentric Kinship: Henry David Thoreau's 'A Plea for Captain John Brown,'" *Southern Speech Communication Journal* 27 (1961): 151–55; Annika Katz, "Slavery and the Development of Thoreau's Social Philosophy," *Moderna Språk* 64 (1970): 327–45; Lauriat Lane, Jr., "Thoreau's Autumnal, Archetypal Hero: Captain John Brown," *Ariel* 6 (1975): 41–48; and Gilman M. Ostrander, "Emerson, Thoreau, and John Brown," *Mississippi Valley Historical Review* 39 (1953): 713–26.

pronouns emphasize that his audience is under direct attack. The audience, Thoreau emphasizes, offends "our nostrils."

In *A Tale of a Tub* Swift pointed out that satire is a glass, a mirror, in which a man sees every face but his own. As these examples from Ruskin and Thoreau reveal, the sage creates a different kind of satire from that found in neoclassical writers, for he in essence grabs the individual members of his audience by the scruff of the neck and forces them to see themselves in his dark mirror.

The Prophet's Warning

In the Old Testament the prophet's chief task involves communicating a divine warning to an erring, disobedient people. As Hosea exclaims, "O Israel, return unto the Lord thy God; for thou hast fallen by thine iniquity" (14:1). Compared to most prophetic warnings, this by Hosea strikes one as rather mild, and Joel, speaking with the words of God, sounds a more strident note: "Blow ye the trumpet in Zion, and sound an alarm in my holy mountain: let all the inhabitants of the land tremble: for the day of the Lord cometh, for it is nigh at hand" (2:1). Micah, who promises dreadful punishment for falling away from the Lord, presents an even more terrifying vision to warn his listeners away from sin: "Hear, all ye people; hearken, O earth, and all that therein is. . . . For, behold, the Lord cometh forth out of his place, and will come down, and tread upon the high places of the earth. And the mountains shall be molten under him, and the valleys shall be cleft, as wax before the fire, and as the waters that are poured down a steep place. For the transgression of Jacob is all this, and for the sins of the house of Israel" (1:2–4). Nonetheless, no matter how terrifying are his visions of punishment, the prophet presents them to offer his listeners one more chance to survive, for his portrayals of a vengeful God paradoxically derive from that God's mercy. According to Ezekiel, the Lord promises, "I will judge you, O house of Israel, every one according to his ways. . . . Repent, and turn yourselves from all your transgressions; so your iniquity shall not be your ruin.... I have no pleasure in the death of him that dieth, saith the Lord God; wherefore turn yourselves, and live ye" (18:30, 32). The prophet's harsh pronouncements offer an undeserved second chance.

This situation in which the prophet, an outsider, comes forth to testify of God's imminent punishment to those in power becomes paradigmatic for Carlyle, who alludes to it frequently. In *Past and Present*, for example, he presents the Peterloo Massacre as a crucial event that prompts the prophet to come forward. This work opens, as we have already observed, with Carlyle pointing to a situation that demands his interpretation, and when it mentions the Peterloo Massacre he repeats the set of techniques with which he began—but with a difference, for he now adds the prophet's warning. First he announces his subject, and then he suggests that something about it is not understood: "Some thirteen unarmed men and women cut down,—the number of the slain and maimed is very countable: but the treasury of rage, burning hidden or visible in all hearts ever since, more or less perverting the effort and aim of all hearts ever since, is of unknown extent." Third, he underlines the importance of the situation by alluding to the Book of Daniel: "In all hearts that witnessed Peterloo, stands written, as in fire-characters, or smoke-characters prompt to become fire again, a legible balance-account of grim vengeance; very unjustly balanced, much exaggerated, as is the way with such accounts: but payable readily at sight, in full with compound interest!" Fourth, he again provides a voice for inarticulate phenomena, in this case for the workers, many of whom lie dead: "And this is what these poor Manchester operatives, with all the darkness that was in them and round them, did manage to perform. They put their huge inarticulate question, 'What do you mean to do with us?' in a manner audible to every reflective soul in this kingdom" (10.16–17). All England heard the question, though few understood it; all England saw the fire-letters, the writing on the wall, though few grasped its meaning. Fifth and finally, the sage warns of imminent, inevitable judgment. "All England heard the question," says Carlyle. "England will answer it; or, on the whole, England will perish" (10.17). This is the basic message of the sage: reform

58

or perish. It is the message, for example, of Ruskin in *The Stones of Venice* and of Thoreau in all his antislavery speeches and essays. Their interpretations, like those of Carlyle, reveal that their contemporaries have abandoned or fallen away from the divine laws that inform the universe and that without such guides they are wandering toward a dreadful destruction.

Carlyle makes the biblical origins of this technique quite clear to his reader, for he points out in detail the situation in which his warning is announced. And the situation is the same, urges Carlyle, with nations. The ancient guides—"Prophets, Priests, or whatever their name"—warned nations when they took the wrong path, but the "modern guides of Nations . . . Journalists, Political Economists, Politicians, Pamphleteers, have entirely forgotten this, and are ready to deny this" (10.28). One cannot deny truth, however, and survive for long. "When a Nation is unhappy, the old Prophet was right and not wrong in saying to it: Ye have forgotten God, ye have quitted the ways of God, or ye would not have been unhappy. It is not according to the laws of Fact that ye have lived and guided yourselves, but according to the laws of Delusion, Imposture, and wilful and unwilful *Mistake* of Fact" (10.28). Pointing out that established authorities have failed to warn his contemporaries, Carlyle justifies his enterprise; pointing out what the prophets did for their people, the spiritual predecessors of his British audience, both indicates the nature of his task and further justifies it. He then uses additional devices to win the audience's favor, making up for the abrasive tone of his warning, a warning that necessarily contains an attack upon his audience, by disclaiming his own responsibility for his dire message: "It is Fact, speaking once more, in miraculous thunder-voice, from out of the centre of the world;—how unknown its language to the deaf and foolish many; how distinct, undeniable, terrible and yet beneficent, to the hearing few: Behold, ye shall grow wiser, or ye shall die! . . . Such is the God's-message to *us*, once more, in these modern days" (10.29–30). It is fact, rather than Carlyle, he claims, that conveys this warning; he is a mere translator. By employing the first-person plural pronoun, he joins with the audience and thus implicitly admits some responsibility for the present situation.[8]

Although both nineteenth- and twentieth-century sages thus speak or write as ventriloquists for mute phenomena, the moderns, who tend to collapse the various parts of the prophetic pattern into one another, rarely make the kind of explicit warnings that Carlyle, Arnold, and Ruskin do. Instead, their often gloomy portraits of contemporary men and mores warn by implication: If you do not change things, these banalities, these horrors, will be even more common in your future than they are now; indeed, they will *be* your future. Didion's "Some Dreamers of the Golden Dream" and "White Album," and Wolfe's "Pump House Gang," "Put-Together Girl," and "Noonday Underground," all accost the reader with representative situations that both permit us to perceive cultural crisis better and warn us about our future.

Visionary Promises

The sage completes the pattern established by Isaiah and other Old Testament prophets by following visionary threats with visionary promises. The fourth chapter of Isaiah promises all the virtuous in Jerusalem, who "shall be called holy" (4:3), that the Lord will "create upon every dwelling place of mount Zion, and upon her assemblies, a cloud and smoke by day, and the shining of a flaming fire by night: for upon all the glory shall be a defence" (4:5), and the thirty-fifth chapter prophesies that the desert will blossom and the blind will see and the lame will rise up restored. Chapter 58 promises the righteous that when they do God's will, "then shall thy light break forth as the morning, and thine health shall spring forth speedily" (58:8). The solacing visions of the Old Testament prophet compensate for his

---

[8]Several times later in *Past and Present*, Carlyle repeats the prophetic pattern, following interpretation and diagnosis by prophetic warning. See, for example, 10.142–44 and 176. His elaborate repetitions of the prophet's warning are well suited to the episodic or segmented structure of prophecy and of course contribute to it.

dire warnings, his visions of peace, security, abundance, and health for those of plague and fire.

In order to complete the prophetic pattern, the secular sages emulate Daniel, Hosea, and Isaiah and offer visions of good that they promise will be fulfilled when their listeners return to the ways of God and nature. For example, Carlyle's "Signs of the Times," which we may take as the first fully developed example of this genre, follows its interpretations, diagnoses, and warnings about the condition of England with words of hope. "We are but fettered," says Carlyle, "by chains of our own forging, and which ourselves also can rend asunder. This deep, paralysed subjection to physical objects comes not from Nature, but from our own un-wise mode of *viewing* Nature" (27.80–81). Even machine and mechanism do not reign supreme, however much they might now afflict and even imprison us: "If Mechanism, like some glass bell, encircles and imprisons us; if the soul looks forth on a fair heavenly country which it cannot reach, and pines, and in its scanty atmosphere is ready to perish,—yet the bell is but of glass; 'one bold stroke to break the bell in pieces, and thou art deliv-ered!'" (27.81) After claiming that his audience can repair the old temples and recover the wisdom and spiritual health of the ancients, Carlyle insists: "Nor are these the mere daydreams of fancy; they are clear possibilities; nay, in this time they are even assuming the character of hopes. Indications we do see in other countries and in our own, signs infinitely cheering to us, that Mechanism is not always to be our hard taskmaster, but one day to be our pliant, all-ministering servant; that a new and brighter spiritual era is slowly evolving itself for all men" (27.81).

In *Past and Present* Carlyle similarly promises his contemporar-ies "a 'Chivalry of Labour,' and an immeasurable Future which it is to fill with fruitfulness and verdant shade," though he admits they now find themselves only standing on the "threshold, nay as yet outside the threshold" (10.277) of such a blessed time. He therefore closes *Past and Present* with a paragraph whose first de-scription of the new labor rises to a visionary crescendo of hope: "noble fruitful Labour, growing ever nobler, will come forth,—the grand sole miracle of Man; whereby Man has risen from the low places of this Earth, very literally, into divine

61

Heavens. Ploughers, Spinners, Builders; Prophets, Poets, Kings; Brindleys and Goethes, Odins and Arkwrights; all martyrs, and noble men, and gods are of one grand Host; immeasurable; marching ever forward since the beginnings of the World. The enormous, all-conquering, flame-crowned Host, noble every soldier in it; sacred, and alone noble" (10.298). This passage exemplifies many of the individual stylistic and rhetorical devices that characterize the sage's prophetic closure. First of all, Carlyle employs a complex sentence structure that builds to a rhetorical climax, and he also makes use of a grammatical series that heaps up examples. In addition, he combines these stylistic and rhetorical patterns with imagery of spiritual progress and the heavens. The dawning of a new day, ascent to heaven, or emphasis upon sun or stars also commonly appear in such closes.

Ruskin, a master of the closing rhetorical flourish, employs many of these devices throughout *Modern Painters*, *The Stones of Venice*, and his other writings. For example, he ends his chapter "Of the Foreground" in the first volume of *Modern Painters* with such a combination of rhetorical climax and closing mention of a star. According to him, everything in nature teaches us the lessons

> that the work of the Great Spirit of nature is as deep and unapproachable in the lowest as in the noblest objects; that the Divine mind is as visible in its full energy of operation on every lowly bank and mouldering stone, as in the lifting of the pillars of heaven, and settling the foundation of the earth; and that to the rightly perceiving mind, there is the same infinity, the same majesty, the same power, the same unity, and the same perfection, manifest in the casting of the clay as in the scattering of the cloud, in the mouldering of the dust as in the kindling of the daystar. (3.492–93)

Ruskin similarly combines his characteristic rhetorical flourishes with such prophetic revelations of God's presence throughout *The Stones of Venice*. A fine example of such prophetic closure appears, for instance, in the last sentences of "The Throne," which opens the second volume. In this chapter he has contrasted conventional attitudes toward Venice with the reality of its humble origins, after which in his role as prophet and sage he points out "the value of the instance thus afforded to us at once of the inscrutableness and the wisdom of the ways of God." If two thousand years ago we could have seen the "slow settling of the slime of those turbid rivers into the polluted sea" and the resulting formation of a "lifeless, impassable, unvoyageable plain," how little we would have understood "the glorious aim which was then in the mind of Him in whose hands are all the corners of the earth! how little imagined that . . . there was indeed a preparation, and *the only preparation possible*, for the founding of a city which was to be set like a golden clasp on the girdle of the earth, to write her history on the white scrolls of the sea-surges, and to word it in their thunder, and to gather and give forth, in world-wide pulsation, the glory of the West and of the East, from the burning heart of her Fortitude and Splendour!" (10.14–15). Thus playing the sage, Ruskin interprets the significance of an apparently unimportant set of islands in the Venetian lagoon. Any historian, or even anyone with anti-quarian interests, could thus have pointed to those islands that provided the first seeds of Venice and its empire. What distin-guishes this passage from such straightforward historical discus-sions, of course, is both that Ruskin finds in these historical facts a divine plan and that he presents his interpretation of it with a dramatic rhetorical flourish alluding to the Bible. As Cook and Wedderburn, Ruskin's editors, point out, the phrase "in whose hands are all the corners of the earth" alludes to Revelation 7:1, and Ruskin uses this allusion as a means of indicating to many of his Victorian readers that they have encountered matters of di-vine law and inspired prophecy. In fact, the crescendo of lush writing to which the sentence builds finds its justification in the supposed fact that it moves from mere earthly historical matters to the divine laws that, Ruskin claims, they embody.

Ruskin, who is never shy about claiming that he can read di-vine intention, frequently ends his chapters with such biblical al-lusion or by pointing to the presence of God. The second volume of *The Stones of Venice* characteristically closes upon such a note. Briefly turning away from his main subject, Ruskin pleads for the preservation of Venice and its works of art, which are threatened by man and time and the elements, and as he so frequently does, he cites his own experience to indicate the value of what his contemporaries allow to be destroyed. He mentions several state rooms in the Ducal Palace

> that were full of pictures by Veronese and Tintoret, that made their walls as precious as so many kingdoms; so precious, indeed, and so full of majesty, that sometimes when walking at evening on the Lido, whence the great chain of the Alps, crested with silver clouds, might be seen rising above the front of the Ducal Palace, I used to feel as much awe in gazing on the building as on the hills, and could believe that God had done a greater work in breathing into the narrowness of dust the mighty spirits by whom its haughty walls had been raised, and its burning legends written, than in lifting the rocks of granite higher than the clouds of heaven, and veiling them with their various mantle of purple flower and shadowy pine. (10.438–39)

Once again, by indicating the presence of God in unexpected places and things, Ruskin produces a positive note on which to close his discussion, for by insisting upon God's role in creating both Venetian art and the origins of the city, he manages to demonstrate what inspiring, what wonderful, things happen when man does not fall away from God but follows the divine within him—as Ruskin claims to do when writing *The Stones of Venice.*

Thoreau uses similar shifts of tone and rhetoric to close his exercises in this form of writing. The lyrical "Walking" concludes with the hope of an earthly Eden: "So we saunter toward the Holy land, till one day the sun shall shine more brightly than ever he has done, shall perchance shine into our minds and hearts, and light up our whole lives with a great awakening light, as warm and serene and golden as on a bankside in autumn" (226). "Slavery in Massachusetts," which is more properly a pronouncement of the sage, uses the beauty of nature to suggest a positive vision and a possible good after much pointed satire and bitter invective.[9] Walking toward a pond, Thoreau

[9]Albert A. Funk, "Henry David Thoreau's 'Slavery in Massachusetts,'" *West-*

confesses that the crimes of his society spoil his pleasure in nature: "Who can be serene in a country where both the rulers and the ruled are without principle? The remembrance of my country spoils my walk. My thoughts are murder to the State, and involuntarily go plotting against her." He then remembers that "the other day" he scented a water lily, "the emblem of purity," which served to show him "what purity and sweetness reside in, and can be extracted from, the slime and muck of earth," and he therefore realizes: "What confirmation of our hopes is in the fragrance of this flower! I shall not so soon despair of the world for it, notwithstanding slavery, and the cowardice and want of principle of Northern men" (108).

"The Last Days of John Brown," which presents the great abolitionist in terms of Christian and even Christic martyrdom, argues that in his death Brown achieved a true victory of the spirit. The essential part of John Brown, claims Thoreau, still remains alive and indeed grows ever stronger throughout the land. Therefore, although he has heard that Brown died on the gallows, he refused and still refuses to believe it:

> On the day of his translation, I heard, to be sure, that he was *hung*, but I did not know what that meant; I felt no sorrow on that account; but not for a day or two did I even *hear* that he was *dead*, and not after any number of days shall I believe it. Of all the men who were said to be my contemporaries, it seemed to me that John Brown was the only one who *had not died*. . . . I never hear of any particularly brave and earnest man, but my first thought is of John Brown, and what relation he may be to him. I meet him at every turn. He is more alive than he ever was. He has earned immortality. He is not confined to North Elba nor to Kansas. He is no longer working in secret. He works in public, and in the clearest light that shines on this land. (152–53)

"A Plea for Captain John Brown," which presents its subject as the contemporary incarnation of Christ, again uses this imagery of visionary promise when Thoreau translates Brown from earth

---

em Speech 36 (1972): 159–68, provides useful background to this work, as do items listed in note 7.

to heaven and from a human being and hero into an angelic presence: "Some eighteen hundred years ago Christ was crucified; this morning, perchance, Captain Brown was hung. These are the two ends of a chain which is not without its links. He is not Old Brown any longer; he is an Angel of Light" (137).

W. E. B. Du Bois ends his chapter on education in *The Souls of Black Folk* (1903) with another common version of the visionary close when he invokes the situation of those who see the Promised Land at a distance. Calling like Matthew Arnold for a "higher individualism which the centres of culture protect," Du Bois suggests that the very sufferings of his people have much to offer the world of culture: "The rich and bitter depth of their experience, the unknown treasures of their inner life, the strange rendings of nature they have seen, may give the world new points of view and make their loving, living, and doing precious to all human hearts. And to themselves in these the days that try their souls, the chance to soar in the dim blue air above the smoke is to their finer spirits boon and guerdon for what they lose on earth by being black." Arguing that the world of culture has no colorline, Du Bois moves from the literal to the symbolic and visionary: "I sit with Shakespeare and he winces not. Across the color line I move arm in arm with Balzac and Dumas, where smiling men and welcoming women glide in gilded halls." Similarly, he can summon Aristotle and Aurelius, who "come all graciously with no scorn nor condescension." Pointing out that thus "wed with Truth, I dwell above the Veil," he turns to white America and asks, "Is this the life you grudge us . . . ? Is this the life you long to change into the dull red hideousness of Georgia? Are you so afraid lest peering from this high Pisgah, between Philistine and Amalekite, we sight the Promised Land?"[10] He alludes to the thirty-fourth chapter of Deuteronomy, in which, before Moses dies, God commands him to ascend Mount Pisgah and there grants him a sight of Canaan as a reward for his loyal service. Throughout the nineteenth century this situation provided a popular subject for hymns and sermons, and it also pro-

---

[10]*The Souls of Black Folk* (New York, New American Library, 1982), pp. 138–39.

vided paradigms, images, and types for a wide range of religious and secular literature.[11] Within these two closing paragraphs Du Bois combines the visionary promise of the Pisgah Sight with the sage's characteristic alternation between vision and satire, for although he does not always write as a sage, he occasionally employs a wide range of the same techniques and allusions. *The Souls of Black Folk* centers on the problem of racial relations in America the same way that Carlyle's *Chartism* and *Past and Present* center on the problem of labor relations in England. Du Bois, who cites Carlyle, clearly knows both his literary techniques and those of the evangelical tradition upon which both men draw. His commitment in this book to rational historical argument produces a work that only occasionally draws on the devices of the sage—and on that account is interesting in our context because it indicates how this genre intermingles with other forms of nonfiction.[12]

The closing paragraph of Arnold's "Function of Criticism at the Present Time" gives the Pisgah Sight another intonation, for he combines a popular evangelical commonplace with references to classical pagan literature. Claiming that Periclean Athens and Elizabethan England, the "epochs of Aeschylus and Shakespeare," possess "the true life of literature," he proclaims: "there is the promised land, towards which criticism can only beckon. That promised land it will not be ours to enter, and we shall die in the wilderness: but to have desired to enter it, to have saluted it from afar, is already, perhaps, the best distinction among contemporaries; it will certainly be the best title to es-

[11]See "The Pisgah Sight—Typological Structure and Typological Image" in Landow, *Victorian Types, Victorian Shadows*, pp. 205–31.

[12]In his ninth chapter, "Of the Sons of Master and Man," Du Bois points out that the economic system of the American south in 1900 was not that of the old industrial north or modern England and France. "It is, rather, a copy of that England of the early nineteenth century, before the factory acts,—the England that wrung pity from thinkers and fired the wrath of Carlyle" (192). The "new captains of industry" (193), often men from the north, turn out to be not the leaders Carlyle had hoped would arise to bring peace and justice to the industrial age, but men who care only for "dollars and dividends" (193). When describing the life of Alexander Crummell in chapter 12, he similarly employs the language, imagery, and rhetoric of *Sartor Resartus*, *On Heroes and Hero-Worship*, and *Past and Present*.

teem with posterity" (3.285). Despite Arnold's rather peculiar critical blindness in failing to notice that his own age, a second renaissance, had achieved literary greatness, he forces us to admire the skill with which he presents his judgments even as we shake our heads in wonderment at his claim that criticism, the criticism he writes, is the finest creation of the age and the one that will be most valued in the future.

Unlike preachers and writers of hymns, who take the Pisgah Sight as a promise of heaven, Victorian writers and artists frequently employ it for its complex mixture of reward and punishment, fulfillment and failure. Elizabeth Barrett Browning's *Aurora Leigh*, her husband's "Pisgah Sights" and other poems, Tennyson's "The Passing of Arthur," Ruskin's *Modern Painters* and *Praeterita*, and Arnold's own "Empedocles on Etna" all manipulate this commonplace type for its built-in ironies. In "The Function of Criticism at the Present Time" Arnold makes a slightly different use of it by situating the promised land in the past as well as in the future. God grants his prophet a sight of Canaan, the land his people will enter after his death, as reward for his obediently leading the obstinate, backsliding Hebrews out of Eygpt and through the desert, but since he does not permit Moses to enter the promised land (as punishment for disobediently striking a desert rock to bring forth water), God blends punishment and reward. Some exegetes, such as the great Evangelical Anglican preacher Henry Melvill, interpreted this incident at least in part to indicate that the Lord desired to show that all men, no matter how blessed or high in position, had to obey His word.[13] Most orthodox students of the Bible, however, concentrated upon the element of promise and took the Pisgah Sight, as it came to be known, as a type of Heaven. Both the type (Canaan) and its fulfillment (Heaven) emphasize futurity, but Arnold sees the "promised land" of culture in the past. True, he implies that such a promised land, such a Canaan of culture, will be entered in the future by another, more fortunate, generation, and he therefore establishes what is essentially a typological

---

[13]Henry Melvill, "The Death of Moses," in *Sermons* (London, 1836), 2: 159–87.

relation between prefiguring Periclean Athens and Elizabethan England and a future England of great culture. At the same time, however, his emphasis upon the pastness of the promised land undercuts this closing promise, perhaps unintentionally.

Coming upon Arnold's mention that "we shall die in the wilderness," one is not at first certain if he draws an analogy between his contemporaries and the Israelites born in slavery who were not fit to enter the promised land or if he intends to establish one between them (or himself) and Moses, the prophet of God and giver of the Law; but his following statement, that they have "saluted it from afar," seems to make clear that he sees his generation—and particularly his own criticism—in the role of Moses, who struggled with a blind, rebellious, benighted people and finally brought them in sight of the promised land, which they then had to attain by their own efforts. Such grandiose self-presentation, which casts the sage in the guise of an inspired prophet, is not at all uncommon in the writings of the Victorian sages. Thoreau thus casts himself as John the Baptist to John Brown's Christ, and Ruskin presents himself, at different times and at different places in his writing, as virtually all the prophets of the Old Testament. What may surprise, of course, is that Arnold, a man deeply suspicious of the Hebraizing Evangelical Protestant tradition, should have drawn upon it both with such skill and with such lack of irony. [14]

Arnold does not always seem to be particularly comfortable using such literary structures drawn from a religious tradition upon which he so looked down, and occasionally he employs them ineffectively. The examples at which we have looked of the way he himself, Ruskin, Carlyle, and Thoreau invoke the full range of prophetic rhetoric suggest that completing the pattern involves more than a closing flourish. In fact, if the would-be sage does not have an adequate vision or promise with which to solace his readers, the attempt at closure falls rather flat, as it does at one point in *Culture and Anarchy*, where Arnold employs

[14]Geoffrey Tillotson notes Arnold's "Puritan passion for what he saw to be best, and missionary passion for making what he saw to be best prevail" in "Matthew Arnold: The Critic and the Advocate," in *Critics and Criticism in the Nineteenth Century* (London, Athlone Press, 1951), p. 60.

a powerful rhetorical climax as he presents his understanding of what will happen when his higher view of culture becomes accepted:

> The moment this view of culture is seized, the moment it is regarded not solely as the endeavour to see things as they are, to draw towards a knowledge of the universal order which seems be intended and aimed at in the world, and which it is a man's happiness to go along with or his misery to go counter to,—to learn, in short, the will of God,—the moment, I say, culture is considered not merely as the endeavour to *see* and *learn* this, but as the endeavour, also, to make it *prevail*, the moral, social, and beneficent character of culture becomes manifest. (5.93)

The problem here lies in the fact that Arnold's progressive movement through higher and higher matters, including "the will of God," ends with an unintentionally comic anticlimax because, rather than stop with some promise of future betterment for his audience, he instead informs them that they will understand that he is right. The fact that the "moral, social, and beneficent character of culture becomes manifest" when his definition of it is accepted hardly justifies the rhetorical fanfare of the sentence. One suspects that Arnold, who was so influenced by Newman and the whole High Church emphasis upon reticence and reserve, found himself unwilling—or unable—to produce the positive vision necessary to complete the structure invoked. Although throughout his career Arnold remained deeply indebted to Thomas Carlyle for individual techniques, general approach, and various major themes, he seems to have been embarrassed by such influence, in large part because he found the self-assertive, openly combative Carlyle uncosmopolitan—too Evangelical, too provincial, and too lower-class.[15]

---

[15]Many students of the Victorian period have taken Arnold's own condescending remarks about Carlyle at face value and assumed that Carlyle's only important influence upon Arnold was to weaken his orthodox religious belief early in his career. But as R. H. Super, Arnold's modern editor, points out, the Carlylean influence was pervasive, though I cannot agree with his conclusion that if Arnold spoke slightingly of Carlyle, "he is merely saying what is clearly enough perceived today: Arnold has survived while Carlyle is unread" (5.414).

Nonetheless, it is from Carlyle that Arnold learned the sage's devices and stance. One can point to other examples of one author's learning the sage's techniques, such as the prophetic pattern, from another. Ruskin, for example, followed Carlyle, particularly in his social criticism, and D. H. Lawrence in turn drew heavily upon Ruskin for his word-painting and manner of self-presentation.[16] But although instances of direct influence, particularly that of Carlyle, appear throughout the nineteenth-century development of this genre, they do not centrally concern us now while we are trying to map the limits of the genre itself. Similarly, although all nineteenth-century practitioners of this form of wisdom literature consciously draw upon the traditions of Old Testament prophecy, such direct indebtedness concerns us only while we observe the genre taking form. Once a genre develops, it assumes a life of its own, and those who come to it after the first generation do not necessarily concern themselves with its roots and sources. The way literary forms thus develop has important consequences for students of literature and literary traditions since it implies that later practitioners of a genre need not have

---

David J. DeLaura, "Arnold and Carlyle," *PMLA* 79 (1964): 104–29, surveys the intellectual relationship between the two men. His classic study, *Hebrew and Hellene in Victorian England: Newman, Arnold, and Pater* (Austin, University of Texas Press, 1969), has demonstrated that Newman, with whom Arnold had a unique intellectual relationship, had by far the more important influence upon him, and I would not wish to deny that obvious fact. What I do want to suggest, however, is that whether or not Arnold admitted or even recognized his debt to Carlyle, he drew upon him for both theme and technique. The following passage from *Culture and Anarchy*, for example, directly derives from Carlyle's redefinition of ideas as machines (because they represent means and not ends) in "Signs of the Times" and other works. Like Carlyle, Arnold also emphasizes the uniqueness of the speaker and the fact that only he possesses an authentic voice. "Faith in machinery is, I said, our besetting danger; often in machinery most absurdly disproportioned to the end which this machinery, if it is to do any good at all, is to serve; but always in machinery as if it had a value in and for itself. What is freedom but machinery? what is population but machinery? what is coal but machinery? what are railroads but machinery? what is wealth but machinery? what are, even, religious organisations but machinery? Now almost every voice in England is accustomed to speak of these things as if they were precious ends in themselves" (5.96).

[16]George P. Landow, "Lawrence and Ruskin: The Sage as Word-Painter," in *Lawrence and Tradition*, ed. Jeffrey Meyers (London, Athlone Press, 1985), pp.

2

Symbolical Grotesques

Grotesque Symbols and Symbolical Grotesques

In the course of interpreting contemporary phenomena, the sage makes extensive use of elaborate symbolical set pieces, some of which he finds in contemporary phenomena and others that he creates from his own imagination. In either case, his practice of relying on complex, often grotesque emblems derives ultimately from both Old Testament prophecy and Victorian biblical interpretation. Carlyle's citation of the death of a malnourished Irish widow in *Past and Present* exemplifies the way the sage's act of interpretation transforms an apparently insignificant event into a grotesque emblem of the condition of the age. Drawing upon William P. Alison's *Observations on the Management of the Poor in Scotland* (1840), Carlyle cites the case of the poor woman who could prove her common humanity to the citizens of a modern city only by infecting them fatally with disease:

A poor Irish Widow, her husband having died in one of the Lanes of Edinburgh, went forth with her three children, bare of all resource, to solicit help from the Charitable Establishments of that

73

City. At this Charitable Establishment and then at that she was refused; referred from one to the other, helped by none;—till she had exhausted them all; till her strength and heart failed her: she sank down in typhus-fever; died, and infected her Lane with fever, so that "seventeen other persons" died of fever there in consequence. The humane Physician asks thereupon, as with a heart too full for speaking, Would it not have been *economy* to help this poor Widow? She took typhus-fever, and killed seventeen of you!—Very curious. (10.149)

Then, continuing to provide a voice for inarticulate fact, Carlyle speaks the meaning contained in the widow's act—indeed, in her very existence. She demands of her fellow creatures that they give her their help and asserts that she deserves it because "I am your sister, bone of your bone; one God made us: ye must help me!" The inhabitants of Edinburgh responded by denying her appeal—"No, impossible; thou art no sister of ours," but as Carlyle emphasizes, she "proves" her sisterhood when her typhus kills them: "They actually were her brothers, though denying it! Had human creature ever to go lower for a proof?" (10.149). In thus demonstrating the relevance of such contemporary phenomena, in thus thrusting upon the audience its need to see deeper into such apparently trivial events, Carlyle becomes a Victorian prophet who reveals that the event to which he directs our attention is a grotesque emblem of the spiritual, moral, and political condition of the age.

His citation of the grotesque, a term that we employ to describe the jarringly unnatural, is completely appropriate for the sage, since his enterprise involves diagnosing instances of disorder. Like other terms in aesthetics and criticism, the grotesque evolved by extrapolating an aesthetic category from what had originally been a stylistic or rhetorical term.[1] Wolfgang Kayser, the leading modern student of grotesque, explains: "By the word

---

[1] For the example of the sublime, which developed from a Longinian term for the high style of writing into an aesthetic category rivaling beauty, see Samuel Holt Monk, *The Sublime: A Study of Critical Theories in XVIII-Century England* (Ann Arbor, University of Michigan Press, 1960), and Marjorie Hope Nicolson, *Mountain Gloom and Mountain Glory: The Development of the Aesthetics of the Infinite* (New York, Columbia University Press, 1963).

grottesco the Renaissance, which used it to designate a specific or-
namental style suggested by antiquity, understood not only something playfully gay and carelessly fantastic, but also something
ominous and sinister in the face of a world totally different from
the familiar one—a world in which the realm of inanimate
things is no longer separated from those of plants, animals, and
human beings, and where the laws of statics, symmetry, and proportion are no longer valid."[2] This second, more threatening
form of the grotesque seems to have taken shape during the six-
teenth century, and although, as Ruskin asserts, the grotesque
has often assumed playful forms during the past two centuries,
the more common, darker kind has commanded most attention
in art, literature, and criticism. In varying degrees all the sages
emphasize that certain monstrous quality of the grotesque
"constituted by the fusion of different realms as well as by a
definite lack of proportion and organization" (24), for their acts
of interpretation, diagnosis, and warning reveal the presence of
disorder in the midst of apparent order. As Kayser points out,
"The grotesque world is—and is not—our own world. The ambiguous way in which we are affected by it results from our awareness that the familiar and apparently harmonious world is alienated under the impact of abysmal forces, which break it up and
shatter its coherence" (37). Within the writings of the sage, the
powerful emphasis upon the grotesque, which in other forms may
appear random, uncaused, or intrinsic to existence, is shown to
derive from the flaws of one's contemporaries: their fusions—or
rather confusions—of moral, political, social, and spiritual order
have rendered reality grotesque. Carlyle's *French Revolution*,
which we may take as a type of such a claim, devotes three volumes to demonstrating how such confusions of order released
abysmal forces, and a large part of the writings of Mailer,
Didion, and Wolfe consists of demonstrations that falling away
from the true path has rendered the age grotesque.

[2]*The Grotesque in Art and Literature*, trans. Ulrich Weisstein (New York,
McGraw-Hill, 1966), p. 21. Hereafter cited in text. Geoffrey Galt Harpham,
On the Grotesque: Strategies of Contradiction in Art and Literature (Princeton,
Princeton University Press, 1982), approaches the grotesque as a confusion in
language categories and as a limit, an outer limit, of the literary.

Kayser urges that the "encounter with madness is one of the basic experiences of the grotesque which life forces upon us" (184), and this encounter, which estranges our world from us, affects us so much because it makes us feel our world is unreliable. Nonetheless, despite all the "helplessness and horror inspired by the dark forces which lurk in and behind our world and have power to estrange it, the truly artistic portrayal effects a secret liberation. The darkness has been sighted, the ominous powers discovered, the incomprehensible forces challenged. And thus we arrive at a final interpretation of the grotesque: AN ATTEMPT TO INVOKE AND SUBDUE THE DEMONIC ASPECTS OF THE WORLD" (188). The sage, who transforms contemporary reality into a grotesque version of itself, or rather who reveals those grotesque aspects of it which his contemporaries fail or refuse to see, thus both summons and triumphs over such demonic forces. He summons them into the presence of his contemporaries by pointing to their existence in one of two ways. Either he shows that some aspect of contemporary reality when seen accurately turns out to be grotesque or he creates a grotesque image or analogy of the age to make its moral and spiritual grotesqueness easier to perceive. Likewise, the sage triumphs over the demonic forces of the grotesque in two ways. First, by explaining its underlying meaning, he makes this threatening disorder a part of greater order. Second, offering his audience a way out of such grotesqueness in the form of visionary promises or positive programs, he similarly controls it.

Carlyle achieves both these effects in his presentation of the Irish widow's death, which he transforms into what Ruskin called a symbolical grotesque, his general term for symbols, allegories, and emblems. This notion of the symbolical grotesque proves particularly useful for understanding the sage's emblematic set pieces, in part because Ruskin's general theories of symbolism and imagination derive chiefly from Old Testament prophecy and in part because they emphasize an intrinsic connection between symbolism, satire, and the grotesque that pervades the writings of the Victorian and modern sages.

The very act of taking such phenomena as the material of interpretation instantly establishes them as matters of importance—and one of the sage's claims is that he perceives signs and warnings overlooked by his fellows. The sage's acts of interpretation also have another significant effect, for they transform some person, thing, or event into an elaborate emblem that the sage explains to his readers or listeners. Furthermore, since these contemporary phenomena that the sage takes to be Signs of the Times function within the prophetic pattern of diagnosis and warning, they reveal major instances of disorder and tend to become grotesque. Since they also provide the sage with means to attack his audience's falling away from the right path, they also tend to become satirical as well.

Before examining the various forms the grotesque assumes in the writings of Victorian and modern sages, I propose to look briefly at Ruskin's writings on the subject, which provide a rare opportunity to observe one of the originators of this literary mode setting forth the theoretical basis of a technique important to it. His discussions of the grotesque have an additional importance to one concerned to comprehend the writings of the sage, for Ruskin relates it to satire and sublimity, fantasy and horror, epistemology and prophecy—to those topics, in other words, which play such an important role in this genre. These explanations appear in the last volume of *The Stones of Venice* (1853) and *Modern Painters*, volume 3 (1856), and take the form of theoretical descriptions of the artist, which are psychological profiles of the mind that creates this artistic mode, and analyses of works of art and literature that embody it. According to the third volume of *Modern Painters*, the grotesque has three basic modes or branches, one of which is the fantastic, a comparatively rare form produced by the "healthful and open play of the imagination" (5.131). This delicate fairy art, which is seen "in Shakespere's Ariel and Titania, and in Scott's White Lady," is seldom achieved, says Ruskin, because the "moment we begin to contemplate sinless beauty we are apt to get serious; and moral fairy tales, and such other innocent work, are hardly ever truly, that is to say, naturally, imaginative; but for the most part laborious inductions and compositions. The moment any real vitality enters them, they are nearly sure to become satirical, or slightly gloomy, and so connect themselves with the evil-enjoying branch" (5.131–32).[3]

The second form of grotesque imagination, which served as the basis for Ruskin's conception of a high art suited to the Victorian age, is the "thoroughly noble one ... which arises out of the use or fancy of tangible signs to set forth an otherwise less expressible truth; including nearly the whole range of symbolical and allegorical art and poetry" (5.132). In explaining this portion of his theory, Ruskin focuses upon the individual image, which he terms the Symbolical Grotesque. According to him, "A fine grotesque is the expression, in a moment, by a series of symbols thrown together in a bold and fearless connection, of truths which it would have taken a long time to express in any verbal way, and of which the connection is left for the beholder to work out for himself; the gaps, left or overleaped by the haste of the imagination, forming the grotesque character" (5.132). Employing Spenser's description of envy in the first book of *The Faerie Queene* as his example of a symbolical grotesque, he demonstrates that it communicates complex truths with more power and economy than can discursive prose. After explaining all the ideas about envy this passage includes, he points out that the poet has compressed all this material in nine lines, "or, rather in one image, which will hardly occupy any room at all on the mind's shelves, but can be lifted out, whole, whenever we want it. All noble grotesques are concentrations of this kind, and the noblest convey truths which nothing else could convey" (5.133). Even the minor examples of this symbolic mode convey truth with a delight "which no mere utterance of the symbolised truth would have possessed, but which belongs to the effort of the mind to unweave the riddle, or to the sense it has of there being an infinite power and meaning in the thing seen, beyond all that is apparent" (5.133).

---

[3]For further discussion of Ruskin's conceptions of fantasy, see George P. Landow, "And the World Became Strange: Realms of Literary Fantasy," in *The Aesthetics of Fantasy Literature and Art*, ed. Roger C. Schlobin (Brighton, England, Harvester, 1982), pp. 105–42. I have discussed Ruskin's ideas of symbolism, imagination, and the grotesque in the contexts provided by his other ideas and the religious background in *The Aesthetic and Critical Theories of John Ruskin* (Princeton, Princeton University Press, 1971).

A few years before he presented this discussion of the grotesque in *Modern Painters*, volume 3, he argued that man's love of symbolism, like his instinctive delight in beauty, derives from fundamental laws of human nature that lead man back to the divine. The last volume of *The Stones of Venice* explains that we experience a sort of "Divine fear" when we perceive that something "is other and greater than it seems," and he speculates that God probably made such recognitions "peculiarly attractive to the human heart" to teach us "that this is true not of invented symbols merely, but of all things amidst which we live; that there is a deeper meaning within them than eye hath seen, or ear hath heard; and that the whole visible creation is a mere perishable symbol of things eternal and true" (11.182–3). Ruskin, whose Evangelical religious heritage continued to color his thought long after he finally abandoned his childhood faith, always believed that the mind first perceives difficult truths in symbolic form. Symbolism, both pictorial and literary, thus has a basic, essential epistemological role.

Ruskin here makes a point that he had learned from his Evangelical upbringing. Eighteenth- and nineteenth-century Bible commentaries, annotated editions of the Scriptures, and sermons all encouraged the Victorian believer to think in terms of symbol and emblem, type and allegory, in large part because they urged that God had created such figures as an efficient means of conveying truth to man's limited faculties. For example, according to the great Evangelical Anglican divine William Romaine,

All our ideas of spiritual objects are comparative, taken from matter, and carried up to spirit. In our present state we have no knowledge but what is first sensible, but what comes into the mind from the senses, and is borrowed from objects upon which they can make their observation.... Scripture knowledge is conveyed in this manner. God accommodates his instruction to our capacities: he makes use of outward and sensible objects to explain inward and spiritual: he applies the book of nature to illustrate the book of grace; thus bringing heavenly things down to the level of our understandings, and setting them (as it were) before our eyes by their natural pictures and just similitudes.[4]

[4]William Romaine, "The Parable of the Dry Bones," *Works*, 6 vols.

79

The enormously popular Baptist preacher Charles Haddon Spurgeon used this accommodationist theory of figurative language, which has a long and honorable history in Western Christianity, as the basis for a theory of homiletic rhetoric and mass communication. Spurgeon, who extends the notion of parable to include other forms of symbol and biblical type, explained to his Victorian audience, "The masses never were, and, perhaps, never will be, able to receive instruction in any other way than by parabolic illustrations. He who would be a successful minister must open his mouth in parables; he who would win the hearts of the multitude must closely imitate his Master, and preach in parables that all men can understand."[5] Pointing out that few men can create effective parables, the great preacher nonetheless reassures his congregation that the Bible both contains many and, "if it be rightly used, is suggestive of a thousand" others. Informing his listeners that he will employ one, he chooses "the parable of the ark" but immediately assures them: "While I do so you must understand that the ark was a real thing—that it really was made to float upon the waters, and carry in it Noah and his family and two of all flesh. This is a fact, not a myth. But I shall take this real fact and use it as a parable." Spurgeon then proceeds to employ the conventional typological interpretation of the ark as a divinely intended prefiguration of the church. "The ark which saved from the floods of water is a beautiful picture of Jesus Christ as the means of salvation, by whom multitudes of all flesh are preserved, and saved from perishing in the floods of eternal perdition." As this example of Spurgeon's transforming a thing or event from biblical history into a "parable" suggests,

---

(London, B. and R. Crosby, 1813), 2: 201. He continues: "While we are here in the body, we have no means of discovering spiritual objects but by divine teaching. God informs us, that such an object in the natural world stands for, as is the perfect representation of, such an object in the spiritual world; and this kind of information he has given us in every Hebrew word: like a parable, it teaches and illustrates heavenly things under the expressive figures of earthly.... The Old Testament, the prophetical writings especially, abound with natural images" (2: 202).

[5]"The Parable of the Ark," *Sermons*, 20 vols. (New York and London, Funk & Wagnalls, 1856), 4: 1. All subsequent quotations from this sermon appear on this and the following page.

such habits of mind derive chiefly from taking the Bible as a series of types and figures of Christ. Typological interpretations, which have as their point of departure the notion that historical facts exist as part of a divine pattern, emphasize, particularly in the Victorian period, the historicity of both type and antitype, the ark and Christ. Both have historical existence. Biblical typology supports emblematic habits of mind by convincing the believer that all facts and events have spiritual meaning. Such interpretive habits and attitudes formed an important part of the intellectual baggage of the original sages and their audience and do much to explain the sage's use of the symbolical grotesque.

The important point for Ruskin is that all symbolism is intrinsically grotesque; according to him, whenever we experience anything too great or too difficult for us to grasp fully—and he holds that most truths are beyond human beings—we encounter the grotesque. *The Stones of Venice* argues that human limitations require the grotesque, which is both the result of man's fallen nature and a divine accommodation to it: "The fallen human soul, at its best, must be as a diminishing glass, and that a broken one, to the mighty truths of the universe round it; and the wider the scope of its glance, and the vaster the truths into which it obtains an insight, the more fantastic their distortion is likely to be, as the winds and vapours trouble the field of the telescope most when it reaches farthest" (11.181). In so far as the imagination perceives truth, the result is "sublime," but "so far as it is narrowed and broken by the inconsistencies of the human capacity, it becomes grotesque" (11.181); and it is rare, he adds, that any exalted truth impresses itself upon the imagination without producing the grotesque. So truth appeared to Moses and the prophets, and so, argues Ruskin, it must still appear to great artists and writers. According to him, in all times and places the grotesque has provided the means by which "the most appalling and eventful truth has been wisely conveyed, from the most sublime words of true Revelation, to the . . . [words] of the oracles, and the more or less doubtful teaching of dreams; and so down to ordinary poetry. No element of imagination has a wider range, a more magnificent use, or so colossal a grasp of sacred truth" (5.134).

81

Symbolical Grotesques

The third form of grotesque imagination, one that is completely grotesque in the usual, narrower sense of the term, arises from the fact that the imagination "in its mocking or playful moods . . . is apt to jest, sometimes bitterly, with under-current of sternest pathos, sometimes waywardly, sometimes slightly and wickedly, with death and sin; hence an enormous mass of grotesque art, some most noble and useful, as Holbein's Dance of Death, and Albert Dürer's Knight and Death, going down gradually through various conditions of less and less seriousness in an art whose only end is that of mere excitement, or amusement by terror" (5.131). According to Ruskin, this darker form of the grotesque includes work ranging from traditional religious images of death and the devil to satire and horrific art, and we may add that it also includes both the more satirical, more conventionally grotesque, interpretive set pieces of the sage and his invented ones as well. Taking quite literally the notion that art and prophecy are closely allied, Ruskin, like Carlyle and many other Victorians, found himself attracted in theory and practice, in his theories of the grotesque and his writings as a sage, to such powerful congeries of types, symbols, and emblems, particularly with a strong tinge of the grotesque as we usually use the term.

Discovered Grotesques

Carlyle, the first of the Victorian sages, liberally salts his works with symbolical grotesques he finds in contemporary phenomena or constructs out of them, and like the Old Testament prophets, he uses such combinations of satire, symbols, and the grotesque to reveal the perilous spiritual condition of his age. Many of these grotesque Signs of the Times turn out to be obviously significant things or events, such as the Peterloo Massacre, but many others, like the Irish widow's death, exemplify matters that received comparatively little public attention. *Past and Present*, which in so many ways can stand as the epitome of this kind of writing, contains another instance of such sordid, disturbing, but seemingly minor phenomena. Here not criminal indifference but a hideous crime is the subject, for Carlyle points to an example of child murder for money as a Sign of the Times that sums up the spiritual state of the modern world:

> At Stockport Assizes,—and this too has no reference to the present state of trade, being of date prior to that,—a Mother and a Father are arraigned and found guilty of poisoning three of their children, to defraud a "burial-society" of some 3*l.* 8*s.* due on the death of each child: they are arraigned, found guilty; and the official authorities, it is whispered, hint that perhaps the case is not solitary, that perhaps you had better not probe farther into that department of things.... It is an incident worth lingering on.... Such instances are like the highest mountain apex emerged into view; under which lies a whole mountain region and land, not yet emerged. (10.4)

Carlyle does not, in the manner of the reporter on the modern tabloid, use such incidents purely to arouse jaded or sick appetites. Rather he finds in such grotesqueness a symbol of the condition of England, a symptom of his age's spiritual and mental state. Carlyle's citation of the Stockport murder, Arnold's mention of similar crimes a decade later, and similar examinations of crime by Truman Capote, Norman Mailer, Joan Didion, and Kate Millett all force the reader to confront hideous evil and attempt to determine if these horrors are truly Signs of the Times.[6] Such examination of grotesque evil plays an important part in the writings of the sage from Carlyle to the present day, for it forces upon the reader the immediate need to understand what is not ultimately understandable—the presence of pain and suffering in human existence. The very horror of such crimes makes them of interest, makes them fascinate, for we feel we must try to understand the apparently meaningless incursion of chaos into everyday life. Such symbolical grotesques inevitably

---

[6]Truman Capote's *In Cold Blood: A True Account of a Multiple Murder and Its Consequences* (1965), Joan Didion's *White Album* (1979), Norman Mailer's *Executioner's Song* (1979), and Kate Millett's *Basement: Meditations on a Human Sacrifice* (1979) stand out as four particularly important works that take such crimes as Carlylean Signs of the Times. Ronald Weber, *The Literature of Fact: Literary Nonfiction in American Writing* (Athens, Ohio University Press, 1980), provides several other important examples.

direct our attention to what are essentially religious questions, but because they appear in a political context, they raise political ones as well. This particular incident of grotesque horror leads Carlyle to raise the question, once again, of what wealth means and to whom it does any good in the modern world.

More than two decades after Carlyle had drawn his audience's attention to child murder for profit, Arnold made use of infanticide as a grotesque emblem of the condition of England. In "The Function of Criticism at the Present Time," which he delivered at Oxford during October 1864, he quoted a newspaper report to deflate English self-satisfaction (and hence demonstrate the need for criticism): "'A shocking child murder has just been committed at Nottingham. A girl named Wragg left the workhouse there on Saturday morning with her young illegitimate child. The child was soon afterwards found dead on Mapperly Hills, having been strangled. Wragg is in custody.'" Arnold points out how "eloquent" is this newspaper account when juxtaposed with the "absolute eulogies of Sir Charles Adderley and Mr. Roebuck.... 'Our old Anglo-Saxon breed, the best in the whole world!'—how much that is harsh and ill-favoured there is in this best! *Wragg!*" (3.273). Arnold's tone makes this citation of child murder an even more aggressive attack upon opposing points of view than Carlyle's had been. Carlyle aimed his discussion of the Stockport murders, however, directly at his audience whereas Arnold directs his at Adderley and Roebuck, thereby permitting his Oxford audience, many of whom were opposed to them, to avoid feeling under attack.

Although the Peterloo riots had an obvious major significance to many of Carlyle's contemporaries and the grotesque incidents at Stockport and Nottingham did not, all three demand some sort of explanation because they so clearly raise major questions about the spiritual and political condition of England. Many of the most effective symbolical grotesques created from contemporary events by Carlyle and other sages, on the other hand, take the form of far more trivial phenomena that are apparently beneath the notice of serious people—at least until the sage turns his attention to them and thereby transforms them into symbolical grotesques. In fact, this identification and subsequent interpretation of trivial phenomena as the embodiments of important truths provides one of the characteristic procedures of both Victorian and modern sages. For example, immediately after Arnold has placed Wragg's act of infanticide next to claims that English stock is the world's finest, he draws attention to precisely such a trivial phenomenon—"the natural growth amongst us of such hideous names,—Higginbottom, Stiggins, Bugg!" According to him, such names imply "a touch of grossness in our race" and an intrinsic, "original shortcoming in the more delicate spiritual perceptions" (3.273). R. H. Super, Arnold's editor, points out that these are names of great antiquity in Britain. Therefore, Arnold's point that they represent something originally present in the nation has some grounds, though his additional claim that the increasing number of people with such names demonstrates essential flaws in the national character seems a trifle foolish and unconvincing.

As this example suggests, such interpretations of the trivial force the writer to take grave rhetorical risks since he can easily lose the confidence of his audience, but they also guarantee that, when successful, the writer will have established his claims to authority and credibility—claims that are essential in an age of transition and shaken belief. By demonstrating to the members of his audience that he can reveal such truth in unexpected places, the sage convinces them to give a hearing to his views of man, society, and culture, which might at first seem eccentric and even insane. Furthermore, by employing apparently trivial phenomena as the stuff of his symbolical grotesques (and their subsequent interpretation), the sage also obtains a ready means of mocking the shortcomings of society.

Past and Present, for instance, employs a series of contemporary facts to create grotesque emblems of what Carlyle finds wrong with nineteenth-century life. "Phenomena," the opening chapter of the third book of *Past and Present*, uses the fact of an "amphibious Pope" to epitomize what has happened to Christianity. When the pope's rheumatism made kneeling during the Corpus Christi processions difficult, his cardinals constructed "a stuffed cloaked figure, of iron and wood, with wool or baked hair; and place[d] it in a kneeling posture. Stuffed figure, or

85

rump of a figure; to this stuffed rump he, sitting at his ease on a lower level joins, by the aid of cloaks and drapery, his living head and outspread hands: the rump with its cloak kneels, the Pope looks, and holds his hands spread; so the two in concert bless the Roman population on *Corpus-Christi* Day, as well as they can" (10.138). According to Carlyle, the pope thus sums up the entire "Scenic Theory of Worship": "Here is a Supreme Priest who believes . . . that all worship of God is a scenic phantasmagory of wax-candles, organ-blasts, Gregorian chants, mass-brayings, purple monsignori, wool-and-iron rumps, artistically spread out,—to save the ignorant from worse" (10.138). Admitting the pope's charities, the bravery of his priests during a recent plague in Naples, and his wish to protect the poor and ignorant from unbelief, Carlyle nonetheless mocks him as an embodiment of "worshipping by stage-machinery" (10.139) in order to protect the established political order from proletarian rage. Such "Gregorian Chant, and beautiful wax-light Phantasmagory" hide "an Abyss, of Black Doubt, Scepticism, nay Sansculottic Jacobinism" (10.139). Carlyle thus reveals that the way the pope's infirmities were accommodated one feast day can tell us what we most need to know about the spiritual and political infirmities of the age as well. His sage's vision has in fact transformed an apparently trivial contemporary phenomenon into a Belshazzar fire-letter that warns his readers that they cannot hope to survive by using an obsolete religion to prop up an obsolete political system.

Such an attack upon the Roman church would have appealed to the many Victorian Protestants who were bitterly hostile to it, and Carlyle's particular harsh criticisms of Catholic pageantry and ritual applied to High Church Anglicanism as well. This symbolical grotesque therefore strikes one as a rather orthodox, if wonderfully effective, piece of satire in which the satirist who writes from the vantage point of society lambasts someone on the fringes. In fact, Carlyle, who writes here as a sage, follows the strategies of the Old Testament prophet and attacks his audience with a second symbolical grotesque. After pointing to the "huge Imposture" (10.140) and obsolete forms represented by the actions of the monarch's champion on Coronation Day, Carlyle directs his reader's attention to the British equivalent of the amphibious pope—"that great Hat seven-feet high, which now perambulates London streets. . . . The Hatter in the Strand of London, instead of making better felt-hats than another, mounts a huge lath-and-plaster Hat, seven-feet high, upon wheels; sends a man to drive it through the streets; hoping to be saved *thereby*" (10.141). Rather than attempting to make better hats, he instead expends all his efforts to persuade others that he has done so. "He too knows that the Quack has become God" (10.141). Unlike the grotesque emblem Carlyle locates in Rome—a grotesque his readers are only too likely to mock as having no relevance to their lot—this London one has no redeeming qualities. The creators of the amphibious pope at least tried to maintain what had once been an effective political and spiritual order in the world, but the creators of the seven-foot hat use such quackery only to make money for themselves. Carlyle therefore finds in this foolish bit of puffery a dreadful warning to his contemporaries: "To me," he says, "this all-deafening blast of Puffery, of poor Falsehood grown necessitous, of poor Heart-Atheism fallen now into Enchanted Workhouses, sounds too surely like a Doom's-blast!" (10.142), and he ends this chapter with the prophet's warning to those who have fallen away from the ways of Truth.

> Oh, it is frightful when a whole Nation, as our Fathers used to say, has "forgotten God"; has remembered only Mammon, and what Mammon leads to! When your self-trumpeting Hatmaker is the emblem of almost all makers, and workers, and men that make anything,—from soul-overseerships, body-overseerships, epic poems, acts of parliament, to hats and shoe-blacking! Not one false man but does uncountable mischief: how much, in a generation or two, will Twenty-seven Millions, mostly false, manage to accumulate? The sum of it, visible in every street, market-place, senate-house, circulating library, cathedral, cotton-mill, and union-workhouse, fills one *not* with a comic feeling! (10.144)

Ruskin similarly employs such "found" grotesques intermingled with the sage's other techniques. For example, in *Unto This Last* he uses a series of these grotesques to question the validity of the

87

way popularized versions of classical economics define *value* and *possession*. Drawing his audience's attention to the embalmed body of St. Carlo Borromeo in Milan Cathedral, Ruskin points out that it holds "a golden crosier, and has a cross of emeralds on its breast" and asks several questions: "Admitting the crosier and emeralds to be useful articles, is the body to be considered as 'having' them? Do they, in the politico-economical sense of property, belong to it? If not, and if we may, therefore, conclude generally that a dead body cannot possess property, what degree and period of animation in the body will render possession possible?" At this point Ruskin cites a second, far more grotesque phenomenon, one taken from contemporary events: "Lately in a wreck of a Californian ship, one of the passengers fastened a belt about him with two hundred pounds of gold in it, with which he was found afterwards at the bottom. Now, as he was sinking—had he the gold? or had the gold him?" (17.86). Here, in brief compass, Ruskin has an emblem of modern society and its relation to its possessions. These satirical grotesques, which play a role in Ruskinian redefinitions of economic terminology, reverberate and expand until they indict an entire society that is hurtling self-destructively into the depths in pursuit of material wealth.[7]

Ruskin, who follows Carlyle in making use of elaborate satirical grotesques created from phenomena encountered in newspaper reports, also develops his own characteristic form based upon landscape description. His elaborate word-painting of La Riccia in the first volume of *Modern Painters* (3.278–80) and that of Torcello in *The Stones of Venice* (10.79–90) exemplify his many transformations of landscape into emblem. But, since we

[7]Thoreau makes a somewhat similar symbolical grotesque out of the fate of an Australian prospector who had discovered an enormous gold nugget: "Howitt says of the man who found the great nugget which weighed twenty-eight pounds, at the Bendigo diggings in Australia:—'He soon began to drink; got a horse and rode all about, generally at full gallop, and when he met people, called out to inquire if they knew who he was, and then kindly informed them that he was "the bloody wretch that had found the nugget." At last he rode full speed against a tree, and nearly knocked his brains out.' I think, however, there was no danger of that, for he had already knocked his brains out against the nugget. . . . He is a type of the class" ("Life without Principle," *Reform Papers*, 163).

shall observe the literary techniques that make up Ruskinian word-painting in chapter 4, "The Sage as Master of Experience," I should here like to widen my range of examples and cite D. H. Lawrence, who learned his word-painting from Ruskin, to exemplify the sage's creation of symbolical grotesques from landscape. In addition to incorporating Ruskinian phenomenological descriptions of the exterior and interior worlds into his writing, Lawrence also employs Ruskinian transformation of natural phenomena into emblems. Lawrence's emblematization of landscape set pieces appears throughout both his travel writing and his fiction. In *Sea and Sardinia*, for example, he presents the solitary figure working within the landscape as an emblem of the old full life, which he contrasts to the life of man under industrialism. He begins, as he so frequently does in such set pieces, by presenting the scene from the vantage point of those moving through a defined space.

> Soon we begin to climb to the hills. And soon the cultivation begins to be intermittent. Extraordinary how the healthy, moor-like hills come near the sea: extraordinary how scrubby and uninhabited the great spaces of Sardinia are. It is wild, with heath and arbutus scrub and a sort of myrtle, breast-high. Sometimes one sees a few head of cattle. And then again come the greyish arable-patches, where the corn is grown. It is like Cornwall, like the Land's End region. Here and there, in the distance, are peasants working on the lonely landscape. Sometimes it is one man alone in the distance, showing so vividly in his black-and-white costume, small and far-off like a solitary magpie, and curiously distinct. All of the strange magic of Sardinia is in this sight. Among the low, moor-like hills, away in a hollow of the wide landscape one solitary figure, small but vivid black-and-white, working alone, as if eternally. There are patches and hollows of grey arable land, good for corn. Sardinia was once a great granary.[8]

Unlike either Ruskin's or Lawrence's own pure word-painting, this passage devotes little effort to presenting visual reality. He briefly mentions an act of vision but does not present visual facts

---

[8]*Sea and Sardinia* (London, William Heinemann, 1956), p. 71. Hereafter cited in text.

of form, color, or brightness in any detail. Instead, the narrating voice simply *names* the objects perceived, after which it comments in some way upon their significance. Although Lawrence organizes the narration of his encounter with the Sardinian landscape in terms of a physical movement through it, he concentrates not as in other places in his writing upon the experience of the visual facts, but rather upon the meaning that these facts have for him. Lawrence, in other words, here emphasizes an act of interpretation rather than one of visual perception.

·Any attempt to present landscape can take three forms—the actual act of perception and the visual experience itself; the primary interpretation of experience (these patches of color are arable fields); and then the political, moral, or philosophical interpretation of this second level (such fields represent man in a natural relation to an unsullied nature).[9] Lawrence, who here concerns himself with the second and third steps almost entirely, thus begins by presenting the action of the climb, then what that act of climbing first reveals—here the fact that cultivated fields become intermittent—after which the describer (or narrator) comments upon the unusual fact that the hills come so close to the sea. He next comments how "scrubby and uninhabited" are Sardinia's great spaces as if to indicate how small a role man has in this world and how little room he and his activities occupy in it. Then, after specifically naming the kind of vegetation that contributes to this overall impression of wildness, Lawrence mentions another visual act: "Sometimes one sees a few head of cattle." Next he compares the scene to the Land's End region of Cornwall, and this mention of native English landscape provides an analogy that makes the Sardinian landscape more understandable. Finally, he arrives at what turns out to be the intellectual center of this passage of description and the purpose to which it has been building: the appearance of solitary human beings working in the midst of this wild, untamed, encompassing nature that no one has yet managed to soil, exhaust, or control.

[9]See Erwin Panofsky, "Iconography and Iconology: An Introduction to the Study of Renaissance Art," *Meaning in the Visual Arts* (Garden City, N.Y., Doubleday Anchor, 1955), which originally appeared as an introduction to *Studies in Iconology* (Oxford, Oxford University Press, 1939).

Immediately after presenting this Wordsworthian vignette, Lawrence makes a sharp contrast between it and scenes one en- counters elsewhere and thereupon draws some culturally significant conclusions about this contrast.

> Usually, however, the peasants of the South have left off the costume. Usually it is the invisible soldiers' grey-green cloth, the Italian khaki. Wherever you go, wherever you be, you see this khaki, this grey-green war-clothing. How many millions of yards of the thick, excellent, but hateful material the Italian Government must have provided I don't know: but enough to cover Italy with a felt carpet, I should think. It is everywhere. It cases the tiny chil- dren in stiff and neutral frocks and coats, it covers their extin- guished fathers, and sometimes it even encloses the women in its warmth. It is symbolic of the universal grey mist that has come over men, the extinguishing of all bright individuality, the blotting out of all wild singleness. Oh, democracy! Oh, khaki democracy! (71)

In addition to possessing the obviously Ruskinian (and Carlylean) contrast of past and present—the one organic and healthy, the other unnatural and destructive—Lawrence's descrip- tion of his climb through the Sardinian hills also makes an essen- tially Ruskinian application of an essentially Ruskinian tech- nique. Like Ruskin he casts himself in the role of the sage who can discern matters of grave importance to his audience in the most unlikely and even apparently trivial contemporary phenom- ena. Like his Victorian forebear, Lawrence proceeds by perform- ing an act of interpretation that transforms these phenomena into an emblem of contemporary spiritual states of mind and soul. Furthermore, like Ruskin, who claimed in *Modern Painters* that his times, not the medieval ones, were the Dark Ages, he points to the way men clothe themselves to suggest how much his contemporaries have lost—how much the age of industrializa- tion has taken from man and his environment.[10]

[10]In the third volume of *Modern Painters* (1856), Ruskin argues that "the title 'Dark Ages,' given to the mediaeval centuries, is, respecting art, wholly in- applicable. They were, on the contrary, the bright ages; ours are the dark ones.... We build brown brick walls, and wear brown coats.... There is,

Invented Grotesques

In contrast to these "found" grotesques that Carlyle and other sages produce by interpreting contemporary phenomena, the "invented" kind take the form of extended analogies, metaphors, and parables they create out of whole cloth. At their simplest, these invented symbolical grotesques appear as witty, often raucous analogies, such as *Chartism*'s description of the impoverished Irishman as a "Sanspotatoe" (29.136).

Past and Present opens with a more extended version of the invented symbolical grotesque. Immediately after announcing the paradox of an England "full of wealth ... dying of inanition," Carlyle describes the condition of England and its workers in terms of baleful enchantment. The work English laborers "have done," says Carlyle, "the fruit they have realised is here, abundant, exuberant on every hand of us: and behold, some baleful fiat as of Enchantment has gone forth, saying, 'Touch it not, ye workers, ye master-workers, ye master-idlers ... ; this is enchanted fruit!'" (10.1). Two million workers find themselves in "Workhouses, Poor-law Prisons; or have 'out-door relief' flung over the wall to them,—the workhouse Bastille being filled to bursting" (10.1–2). These workers, some of the finest in the world, sit there imprisoned "as in a kind of horrid enchantment; glad to be imprisoned and enchanted, that they may not perish starved." Citing the words of a picturesque tourist of his own imagining, Carlyle describes the interior of such a workhouse Bastille and the silent despair of its inhabitants, which he interprets: "An Earth all lying round, crying, Come and till me, come and reap me;—yet we here sit enchanted!" (10.2). At the heart of this Carlylean grotesque emblem of the condition of England resides a simple conceit, heavy with implicit satire, which we can state in the following terms: British workers, the best in the world, find themselves helpless and unable to work when so much work is to be done; surely only evil magic, only enchant-

---

however, also some cause for the change in our own tempers. On the whole these are much *sadder* ages than the early ones; not sadder in a noble and deep way, but in a dim wearied way,—the way of ennui, and jaded intellect, and uncomfortableness of soul and body" (5.321).

ment, only a curse could have produced such an absurd, inefficient, essentially unjust state of affairs. Only something like "Enchantment" could explain what has gone wrong. Only enchantment could explain why "we have more riches than any Nation ever had before; we have less good of them than any Nation ever had before," and worse, worse indeed: "In the midst of plethoric plenty, the people perish; with gold walls, and full barns, no man feels himself safe or satisfied. Workers, Master Workers, Unworkers, all men, come to a pause; stand fixed, and cannot farther. Fatal paralysis spreading inwards, from the extremities, in St. Ives workhouses, in Stockport cellars, through all limbs, as if towards the heart itself." Is this no mere analogy, no mere fable, then? "Have we," asks Carlyle, "actually got enchanted, then; accursed by some god?—" whereupon he closes this first chapter of *Past and Present*, which he has called "Midas," with a symbolical grotesque in the form of the old Greek fable of the greedy king that answers his question and thereby explains precisely what kind of enchantment Britain has brought upon itself: "Midas longed for gold, and insulted the Olympians. He got gold, so that whatsoever he touched became gold,—and he, with his long ears, was little the better for it.... What a truth in these old Fables!" (10.6). Britain, as the rest of *Past and Present* demonstrates, has given itself up to the pursuit of material wealth and thus managed to destroy all capacity to enjoy it.

Interpretation, diagnosis, and warning all appear in this Carlylean progression of symbolical grotesques. Having thus introduced the conceits of enchantment, Midas, and workhouse Bastille, Carlyle repeatedly employs them as mock-explanatory devices throughout the volume, and he also connects them to his found grotesques, such as that created by the Stockport child murders, the presentation of which immediately follows that of baleful Enchantment.

Given Carlyle's major emphasis upon fact, most of his symbolical grotesques, such as the amphibious pope and "that great Hat seven-foot high, which now perambulates London streets," in *Past and Present*, obviously derive from contemporary phenomena, but he occasionally employs the invented form of the sym-

bolical grotesque with particular brilliance as well. Such invented
grotesques play a greater role in the writings of Ruskin and Arnold. Ruskin's description of the "Goddess of Getting-on" in
"Traffic" and Arnold's analysis of England's Barbarians, Philistines, and Populace in the third chapter of *Culture and Anarchy*
exemplify some of the most brilliant satiric emblems of the sage.
In his writings on political economy Ruskin makes major use of
them, and they effectively replace the word-painting that characterizes his art criticism as a favorite rhetorical device. Ruskin's invented symbolical grotesques, which take several chief forms, are
particularly useful in summing up the flaws in opposing positions.
These little satiric narratives and analogies of course owe much
to neoclassical satirists, particularly Swift, whose *Tale of a Tub*
and *Gulliver's Travels* make extensive use of elaborate analogies
to cast an opposing view in a poor light.

In "Traffic" Ruskin mocks his audience's conception of an ideal
life by presenting it in the form of what is essentially a dream vision. Arguing that his listeners' worship of the Goddess of Getting-on implies they also condemn others to miserable lives, he
presents a picture of their ideal that enforces corollaries or implicit points they would willingly leave out of their sight and
consciousness.

> Your ideal of human life then is, I think, that it should be passed
> in a pleasant undulating world, with iron and coal everywhere be-
> neath it. On each pleasant bank of this world is to be a beautiful
> mansion, with two wings; and stables, and coach-houses; a moder-
> ately-sized park; a large garden and hot-houses; and pleasant car-
> riage drives through the shrubberies. In this mansion are to live
> the favoured votaries of the Goddess; the English gentleman, with
> his gracious wife, and his beautiful family; he always able to have
> the boudoir and the jewels for the wife, and the beautiful ball
> dresses for the daughters, and hunters for the sons, and a shooting
> in the Highlands for himself. At the bottom of the bank, is to be
> the mill; not less than a quarter of a mile long, with one steam en-
> gine at each end, and two in the middle, and a chimney three
> hundred feet high. In this mill are to be in constant employment

from eight hundred to a thousand workers, who never drink, never strike, always go to church on Sunday, and always express themselves in respectful language. (18.453)

As Ruskin points out, this image of human existence might appear "very pretty indeed, seen from above; not at all so pretty, seen from below," since for every family to whom the Englishman's deity is the Goddess of Getting-on, one thousand find her the "Goddess of *not* Getting-on" (18.453). By making explicit the implications of such a vision of life based upon an ideal of competition, this symbolical grotesque serves a powerful satiric purpose. Ruskin's expertise as an art critic here turns out to be particularly helpful, for he carefully explains the sketched-in elements of his supposedly ideal scene with the same skill that he uses in setting forth his descriptions of Alpine landscape, the city of Venice, or Turner's paintings. In each case he proceeds by presenting visual details and then drawing attention to their meaning. Here he first presents, slightly tongue-in-cheek, an image of the English capitalist's Earthly Paradise, and then, once he has sketched it for his audience, he presents its dark implications by showing the world of have-nots upon which it sits both literally and symbolically. By moving through his created word-picture from upper to lower, he endows each portion of his visual image with a moral and political valuation: the upper classes reside literally, spatially, above the industries that provide their wealth and also above the workers who slave to make their lives ones of ease.

A second form of the invented symbolical grotesque, the one that takes the form of a brief narrative, also appears in "Traffic." When Ruskin argues against those who claim that they cannot afford to create beautiful surroundings for human life, he employs a characteristic parable to reduce such opposing claims to absurdity. Suppose, he instructs his listeners, that he had been sent for "by some private gentleman, living in a suburban house, with his garden separated only by a fruit wall from his next door neighbour's" (18.438) to advise him how to furnish his drawing-room. Finding the walls bare, Ruskin suggests rich furnishings, say fresco-painted ceilings, elegant wallpaper, and damask curtains, and his client complains of the expense, which he cannot afford. Pointing out that his client is supposed to be a wealthy man, he is told:

> "Ah yes," says my friend, "but do you know, at present, I am obliged to spend it nearly all on steel-traps?" "Steel-traps! for whom?" "Why, for that fellow on the other side of the wall, you know: we're very good friends, capital friends; but we are obliged to keep our traps set on both sides of the wall; we could not possibly keep on friendly terms without them, and our spring guns. The worst of it is, that we are both clever fellows enough; and there's never a day passes that we don't find out a new trap, or a new gun-barrel, or something." (18.438–39)

Fifteen million a year, his client tells Ruskin, the two good neighbors spend on such traps, and he doesn't see how they could do with less, and so Ruskin the room decorator must understand why so few resources exist to beautify his client's environment. Turning to his audience, Ruskin abandons the pose of the naif and comments in the tones of the Old Testament prophet: "A highly comic state of life for two private gentlemen! but for two nations, it seems to me, not wholly comic." Bedlam might be comic, he supposes, if it had only one madman, and Christmas pantomines are comic with one clown, "but when the whole world turns clown, and paints itself red with its own heart's blood instead of vermilion, it is something else than comic, I think" (18.278).[11] Having first mocked with his satirical parable the intellectual seriousness of his listeners' self-justifications for failing to spend money on beautifying their environments, Ruskin next moves from mocking to damning them. In the manner of the Old Testament prophet he demonstrates that the actions of his contemporaries reveal that they have abandoned the ways of God and are inevitably heading toward a terrible destruction.

Like most other techniques of the sage, this Ruskinian parable

---

[11]Ruskin echoes, possibly consciously, Carlyle's close to "Phenomena" in *Past and Present*, which comments that the sum of Mammon-worship "visible in every street, market-place, senate-house, circulating library, cathedral, cotton-mill, and union-workhouse, fills one *not* with a comic feeling!" (10.144)

serves multiple functions: It simultaneously interprets the dullness of English design in terms of the nation's political, economic, and military choices and satirizes England and the English; it diagnoses his nation's ills, explains how they came about, and threatens worse disaster if proper actions are not taken; it contributes to Ruskin's position or pose as a wisdom-speaker and hence adds to his ethos; and it creates a self-contained section or episode that can convince readers even if they reject Ruskin's other points in "Traffic."

Such self-contained parables, sections, and arguments typify the writing of the sage and create its characteristic discontinuity. On the one hand, this discontinuous, segmented form obviously derives from Old Testament prophecy. On the other, it is the product of romanticism's emphasis upon lyric moments and upon moments of intense experience and intense expression.[12] Romanticism's emphasis upon these lyric bursts and visionary tableaux, a result or possibly source of making the lyric the central form of the age, creates major problems for writers and readers, and one of the most noticeable of these was the loss of ability to read epic and similar long forms properly. Croce's reading *La Divina Commedia* as an assemblage of lyric poems and brief narratives and several generations of critics' mishandling of *Paradise Lost* show one of the consequences of such elevation of lyric to a dominant form, and the British romantic poet's general lack of success with the long forms embodies another. One genre in which nineteenth-century authors from Carlyle onward managed to solve the problems posed by such an emphasis upon intense passages (whether of satire or of vision) is that composed by the writings of the sage. In this form, which already takes great rhetorical risks, formal unity is often a matter of repetition and trains of imagery and paradigms, and the discontinuity, which elsewhere hinders success, here proves to promote it. The genre's rapid shifts of tone, abrupt change of vantage point, and alternation of satire and vision all lend themselves to more or less self-contained minor structures within the entire work. Within this

---

[12]M. H. Abrams, *The Mirror and the Lamp: Romantic Theory and the Critical Tradition* (New York, Oxford, 1953), contains the classic statement of such effects of critical attitudes upon literature. See especially pp. 70–138.

kind of aesthetic, such compartmentalization proves an advantage because if the sage fails to convince in one section, the separation between parts serves to provide an almost entirely fresh start. Since the sage strives chiefly to change the way his audience perceives various matters, any single success in this enterprise can carry the day.

The effectiveness of the invented symbolical grotesque as an argumentative device appears with particular clarity in Matthew Arnold's mocking division of the English into three groups or classes: Barbarian, Philistine, and Populace.[13] In presenting his set of analogies, all of which are closely related to satiric definitions and descriptions, Arnold claims that the British aristocracy is most accurately designated as the Barbarians.

> The Barbarians, to whom we all owe so much, and who reinvigorated and renewed our worn-out Europe, had, as is well known, eminent merits; and in this country, where we are for the most part sprung from the Barbarians, we have never had the prejudice against them which prevails among the races of Latin origin. The Barbarians brought with them that staunch individualism, as the modern phrase is, and that passion for doing as one likes, for the assertion of personal liberty, which appears to Mr. Bright the central idea of English life, and of which we have, at any rate, a very rich supply.... The care of the Barbarians for the body, and for all manly exercises; the vigour, good looks, and fine complexion which they acquired and perpetuated in their families by these

---

[13]R. H. Super points out that the "terminology and ideas" of *Culture and Anarchy*, today Arnold's best-known work, "are usually taken as central to his thinking" (5.416), so that an account of criticism of them is almost an account of Arnold criticism in general. Arnold's terminology, its sources, and the context of his argument are discussed in, for example, Sidney Coulling, *Matthew Arnold and His Critics: A Study of Arnold's Controversies* (Athens, Ohio University Press, 1974); David J. DeLaura, *Hebrew and Hellene in Victorian England* (Austin, University of Texas Press, 1969); John Holloway, *The Victorian Sage: Studies in Argument* (London, Macmillan, 1953); Park Honan, *Matthew Arnold: A Life* (New York, McGraw-Hill, 1981); Patrick J. McCarthy, *Matthew Arnold and the Three Classes* (New York, Columbia University Press, 1964); Lionel Madden, *Matthew Arnold: A Study of the Aesthetic Temperament* (Bloomington, Indiana University Press, 1967); Lionel Trilling, *Matthew Arnold*, Uniform Edition of the Works (New York, Harcourt Brace Jovanovich, 1977); and Fred G. Walcott, *The Origins of "Culture and Anarchy": Matthew Arnold and Popular Education in England* (Toronto, University of Toronto Press, 1970).

means,—all this may be observed still in our aristocratic class. (5.140–41)

Unfortunately, whatever culture the Barbarians possessed was largely external and "consisted principally in outward gifts and graces, in looks, manners, accomplishments, prowess" (5.141). Even their inward gifts, claims Arnold, were chiefly those that come nearest to outward ones—courage, a high spirit, and self-confidence. Having, like Carlyle, juxtaposed past and present, Arnold then points out the basic similarities of the aristocratic classes then and now, for, he claims, even making "allowances for the difference of the times, surely we can observe precisely the same thing now in our aristocratic class. In general its culture is exterior chiefly; all the exterior graces and accomplishments, and the more external of the inward virtues, seem to be principally its portion" (5.141).

Against the Barbarians, who stand for the aristocracy, Arnold places the Philistines, a term that for him incorporates both the middle and the working classes. As he explains, that part of the working classes

which gives all its energies to organising itself, through trades' unions and other means, so as to constitute, first, a great working-class power independent of the middle and aristocratic classes, and then, by dint of numbers, give the law to them and itself reign absolutely,—this lively and promising part must also, according to our definition, go with the Philistines; because it is its class and its class instinct which it seeks to affirm—its ordinary self, not its best self; and it is a machinery, an industrial machinery, and power and pre-eminence and other external goods, which fill its thoughts, and not an inward perfection. (5.142–43)

Only that "raw and half-developed" part of the working classes that has long lain submerged in "poverty and squalor" (5.143) falls within the category designated as the Populace, and Arnold concentrates upon the first two groups.

As Super points out in his annotations to *Culture and Anarchy*, Arnold first describes the English aristocracy as Barbarians in the closing section of the preface to *Essays in Criticism*, which quotes a line from Byron's *Childe Harold's Pilgrimage* that comments on the aristocracy at Oxford: "There are our young barbarians, all at play!" (3.290) The same passage mentions the Philistines, a mocking term Arnold borrowed from the German romantics and discussed at length in "Heinrich Heine" (3.111–13). The point here of course is not that Arnold drew upon others for his famous categories but that he made of them wonderfully effective satiric and analytic tools that propel his polemic against complacency and its corollary neglect of culture and true self-development. Arnold explained to his mother that "the merit of terms of this sort is that they fix in people's minds the *things* to which they refer" (5.415). Like Carlyle, whose attack upon middle-class complacency with the words *gig* and *gigamanty* Arnold mentions in "Heinrich Heine," he creates idiosyncratic terms that function as grotesque satirical emblems and then organizes his argument in terms of them.

A passage in Thoreau's "Walking," which contains redefinition, social criticism, a visionary moment, and bitter satire, demonstrates both how rich and varied a symbolical grotesque can be and also how effectively it can sum up the concerns of an entire work. Thoreau begins with a simple declarative sentence that serves to redefine a term beloved of materialist society in his age and our own: "Nowadays almost all man's improvements, so called, as the building of houses and the cutting down of the forest and of all large trees, simply deform the landscape, and make it more and more tame and cheap." The next sentence makes a sharp contrast to this declarative one by calling for an improvement by his contemporaries—literally for a new people, a new and higher race of beings who could appreciate nature: "A people who would begin by burning the fences and let the forest stand!" Then after this clause, which essentially states a prayer for the future, Thoreau plunges us directly into a visionary world in the manner of Isaiah and St. John.

> I saw the fences half consumed, their ends lost in the middle of the prairie, and some worldly miser with a surveyor looking after his bounds, while heaven had taken place around him, and he did

100

not see the angels going to and fro, but was looking for an old post-hole in the middle of Paradise. I looked again, and saw him standing in the midst of a boggy Stygian fen, surrounded by devils, and he had found his bounds without a doubt, three little stones, where a stake had been driven, and looking nearer, I saw that the Prince of Darkness was his surveyor. (199)

Like the millenarians who were so popular throughout much of the nineteenth century, he opens his thumbnail vision with the beginnings of heaven on earth, after which he satirically places a "worldly miser" in the midst of this transformation.[14] The scene changes, and the worshiper of Mammon who violates the earth and destroys its blessed wildness has found his place in hell—and with him so have all members of his readership who fail to recognize that the earthly paradise already exists in wild nature.

Twentieth-Century Grotesques

The use of such symbolical grotesques by the sage to provide the climax of argument and satiric attack continues in the twentieth century. Mailer brilliantly creates a modern grotesque in "Some Origins of the Fire" when he describes how he stood in line for almost an hour while waiting for a cold drink in the Florida heat. As he proceeds to describe the inadequacies of mechanical solutions to creature comforts, he indicts his society, for, a true descendant of Carlyle, Ruskin, and Arnold, he perceives and fears the extent to which modern society has become mechanical. He fears this domination of the machine particularly because he perceives that such domination has rendered man himself mechanical and inhumane. Since the main purpose of this history of the first voyage to the moon is to explore the possibilities of human heroism and the human ideal in an age of technology, such a set piece reverberates throughout the volume. Mailer begins by setting the scene: "In back of the Press Site,

---

[14]For discussions of the effect of the Apocalypse upon Victorian literature, see note 13 above.

more than a hundred radio and TV trailers were now arrayed behind one another in ranks and rows of huge white ruminants,
the very sacred cows of American technology. Yet there was only
one trailer reserved for food" (91). Admitting that it "was next
to heartwarming" to discover a piece of poor planning amid the
"icy efficiencies" of NASA, he describes the grotesque results of
placing one's faith in machines when it should be placed in men.

> The trailer was inadequate to the needs of the Press—over a hun-
> dred waited in line, more than a hundred walked away in disgust.
> The line drifted forward about as fast as a tide works up a beach.
> The trailer interior consisted of a set of vending machines for chili-
> burgers, hamburgers, pastries—all people wanted were cold drinks.
> So the line crawled, while everyone waited for the same machine.
> Nobody was about to have machine-vended chiliburgers at half-
> past eight in the morning. But so many demands on the iced-drink
> machine caused malfunctions. Soon, two vending machine workers
> were helping to service the machine. Still it took forever. Coins
> had to go into their slot, change be made, cups filled, tot of
> cracked ice dropped, syrup poured, then soda. Just one machine. It
> was pure American lunacy. Shoddy technology, the worst kind of
> American shoddy, was replacing men with machines which did not
> do the work as well as the men. This crowd of a hundred thirsty
> reporters could have been handled in three minutes by a couple of
> countermen at a refreshment stand in a ball park. But there was an
> insidious desire to replace men everywhere with absurd machines
> poorly designed and abominably put together; yes, this abominable
> food vending trailer was the proper opposite number to those smug
> and complacent VIPs in their stands a half mile away; this was the
> world they had created, not the spaceship. (91–92)

Thus, what begins as a small-minded complaint about some trivial personal discomfort that the writer has experienced soon
metamorphoses into a type, a representative example of underlying laws and rules that can serve as a door to greater understanding. The comical situation quickly changes before our eyes into
an emblem of what is wrong with our society. Like Carlyle and
his many nineteenth-century heirs, Mailer draws his reader's attention to an apparent triviality which he first reveals to be one

of the Signs of the Times and then proceeds to explain. The very metamorphosis of the event into something worthy of consideration and interpretation makes it a device characteristic of the sage. Mailer demonstrates to the reader not only that such apparent trivialities contain essential truths but also that he, Mailer as exegete and bearer of wisdom, is the only one who can perceive them.

Furthermore, Mailer demonstrates that the phenomenon he choses to present to the reader in all its grotesque significance proves not merely meaningful, not merely something that bears significance, but rather something that stands as a synecdoche of the society as a whole, for according to him the absurd scene, in which two men who could easily serve the one hundred reporters far better and more humanely than any machine, instead serve as acolytes to an inefficient machine, reveals a flaw of American society. It reveals, in other words, the way Americans (or at least Americans in authority) have placed their faith in machines rather than in human beings when such allegiance turns out to be particularly, absurdly, grotesquely inappropriate.

Such an emblem of American reliance upon shoddy technology threatens to demonstrate that the entire attempt to voyage to the moon is equally absurd since it obviously embodies American faith in technology. But Mailer, perhaps to our surprise, given the opening of this book, does not elect to make the soft-drink machine represent the forces that have created the moon shot. No, instead he distinguishes between good and bad technology—between that technology which fails to improve the lives of people and that which serves them. What makes the technology behind the moon voyage so privileged for Mailer, so different from that embodied in the soft-drink machine's grotesque inappropriateness, is simply that it permits people to test themselves, to search for the limits of human capacity—in a phrase, to explore the nature and limits of humanity.

Near the opening of *Of a Fire on the Moon*, he posed one of the problems the book would survey when he admitted "that he hardly knew whether the Space Program was the noblest expression of the Twentieth Century or the quintessential statement of our fundamental insanity" (15). When presenting the soft-drink trailer as what I have termed a symbolical grotesque, Mailer aligns the "lunacy" that created this inefficient way to serve human needs with what he finds wrong with America and the modern world but, pointedly, he does not align it with the space program.

Considering this instance of the symbolical grotesque within the context of the entire book, we perceive that Mailer has managed to distinguish two basic forms of American technology and assign value to each. In so doing he also manages to convince us that he has perceived a central fact about America—that he has, in fact, properly perceived and read the Signs of the Times. Further, he convinces us that whatever value he may finally discover in the moon voyage itself will not turn out to be the same as that embodied in shoddy technology. The machine, in other words, takes various forms, not all of which threaten human life.

Like Mailer, Didion chooses particularly grotesque phenomena as Signs of the Times. And like Carlyle, she reveals both the representative and grotesque qualities of a religious figure as part of her knife thrust at the heart of the age. In "James Pike, American" she presents a lapsed Episcopalian bishop as her predecessor presents the amphibious pope—that is, as the embodiment of the grotesque spiritual ills of the age. She finds him, first of all, "a character so ambiguous and driven and revealing of his time and place that his gravestone in the Protestant Cemetery in Jaffa might well have read only JAMES PIKE, AMERICAN" (*White Album*, 53). Pike represents to Didion modern amorality, for this once-bishop of California was a man who, she emphasizes, felt himself bound to no oath and no responsibility. For example, "he invented an ecclesiastical annulment to cover his divorce from 'his first wife' Jane, although no such annulment was actually granted. 'In his mind,' his biographers explain, 'the marriage was not merely a mistake, but a nullity in the inception.' In his mind. He needed to believe in the annulment because he wanted to be Bishop of California" (55–56). Didion relates that she first encountered Pike's approach to life and religion in his pastoral tract *If You Marry outside Your Faith*, "and I was struck dumb by Bishop Pike's position, which appeared to be that I had

not only erred but had every moral right and obligation to erase
this error by regarding my marriage as null, and any promises I
had made as invalid. In other words the way to go was to forget
it and start over" (56). As she concludes, here was a man who
believed that the world could be reinvented whenever such
would convenience us, a man who felt no responsibility to anything but his present need—and yet (and this is what makes him
a Representative Man) who considered himself a spiritual leader.
"Here was a man," Didion marvels, "who moved through life believing that he was entitled to forget it and start over, to shed
women when they became difficult and allegiances when they became tedious and simply *move on*, dismissing those who quibbled
as petty and 'judgmental' and generally threatened by his superior
and more dynamic view of human possibility" (57). As she concludes, Pike's belief that "the world can be reinvented smells of
the Sixties in this country, those years when no one at all
seemed to have any memory or mooring" (57–58). Like Carlyle's
pope, Didion's bishop embodies the spiritual disease of the age
and as such stands forth a pathetically grotesque Sign of the
Times.[15]

If her discussion of Bishop Pike reminds us of Carlyle's earlier
treatment of George Hudson, a stock swindler he made the subject of one of the *Latter-Day Pamphlets*, that of the vulgar late-
nineteenth-century mansions in "The Seacoast of Despair" reminds us of Ruskin's *Stones of Venice* and "Traffic," in part
because Didion repeats the Ruskinian strategy of using a nation's
taste as an index to its spiritual state and also because she alludes
directly to the Victorian sage.[16] Throughout this brief piece

[15]Such use of individual people as symbolic grotesques appears elsewhere
throughout her work. For example, in *Slouching towards Bethlehem*, she had earlier treated Michael Laski as such a symbolic type in "Comrade Laski C. P. U.
S. A. (M.-L.)" and Howard Hughes as one in "7000 Romaine, Los Angeles
38." She concludes that we dwell upon Hughes because he reminds us that "the
secret point of money and power in America is neither the things that money
can buy nor power for power's sake . . . , but absolute personal freedom, mobil-
ity, privacy" (71).

[16]Similarly, Tom Wolfe's *Painted Word* (1975) and *From Bauhaus to Our
House* (1982) both follow the Ruskinian tradition. *The Painted Word*, like much
of *Modern Painters*, attacks established critics for blindness and pretentiousness,
while *From Bauhaus to Our House* follows both *The Stones of Venice* and *The*

Didion points to the meaning and significance of the worship of Mammon. According to Didion, "Newport is the monument of a society in which production was seen as the moral point, the reward if not exactly the end, of the economic process. The place is devoid of the pleasure principle" (*White Album*, 210). Thus far she makes her points much in the manner of the great Victorian creators of this genre, but when she proceeds to examine the life led within these houses, she makes a woman's criticism of it. She points out that although these lavishly decorated mansions would at first seem to have been the province of women and their very reward for having attained the status of wife to a Captain of Finance and Industry, in fact the very opposite is the case: these are men's houses in which women have only an illusory freedom. Furthermore, "the very houses are men's houses, factories, undermined by tunnels and service railways, shot through with plumbing to collect salt water, tanks to store it, devices to collect rain water, vaults for table silver, equipment inventories of china and crystal and 'Tray cloths—fine' and 'Tray cloths—ordinary'" (212). These mansions are great machines which crush rather than free their occupants. "The mechanics of such houses take precedence over all desires or inclinations; neither for great passions nor for morning whims can the factory be shut down, can production—of luncheons, of masked balls, of *marrons glacés*—be slowed" (212). Newport turns out to be "homiletic," according to Didion. It turns out to be "a fantastically elaborate stage setting for an American morality play in which money and happiness are presented as antithetical." The builders of these mansions "had apparently dreamed the dream and made it work. And what they did then was to build a place which seems to illustrate, as in a child's primer, that the production ethic led step by step to unhappiness, to restrictiveness, to entrapment in the mechanics of living. In that way the lesson of Bellevue Avenue is more seriously radical than the idea of Brook Farm. Who could fail to read the sermon in the stones of Newport?" (213). Or perhaps

---

Seven Lamps of Architecture in attacking contemporary architects for incompetence, ignorance of the past, and false professionalism.

we should say, who, now that Didion has instructed us, could fail to find this sermon there?

Comparing the way Tom Wolfe and Germaine Greer turn similar phenomena into symbolical grotesques tells us much about the use of this device of the sage in other related forms of contemporary nonfiction. In *The Pump House Gang* (1968) and other early writings, Wolfe constructs entire essays—he calls them "stories" in the first sentence of his introduction—upon a single grotesque phenomenon that he makes a Sign of the Times. "The Put-Together Girl," for instance, takes the form of a profile of Carol Doda, a dancer in a San Francisco nightspot who acquired a brief moment of notoriety by having her breasts injected with silicone until they ballooned into a technological parody of female secondary sexual characteristics. Wolfe begins his examination of what happens when one violates nature by describing Doda in a particularly appropriate setting, the stunted urban landscape that both provides the background for her daily life as a nightclub entertainer and also embodies the essential problems of which she is a living emblem. Wolfe begins, therefore, on San Francisco's Broadway, a section of which contains the city's "skin-show nightclubs, boho caves . . . and 'colorful' bars with names like Burp Hollow. There is one tree on Broadway. It is about three inches in diameter, about 12 feet tall, and has 342 minute leaves on it and a tin anti-urine sleeve around the bottom. Carol Doda was standing under this tree as if it could hide her" while someone tries to get her a cab.[17] She cannot stand out in the street and signal one herself, because "there is no telling what would happen or how many flaming nutballs would stop or—who the hell knows what?—because of 'them,' *them* being her breasts" (83). Writing without the magisterial tone and diction of the Victorian sages, Wolfe adopts those of the people he is dissecting and alternates between a fairly formal analytic prose spiced by a few words or terms employed by his subjects and one learned from Joyce, Woolf, and Faulkner that he uses to get inside their consciousness, often so he can at the

[17]*The Pump House Gang* (New York, Farrar, Straus and Giroux, 1968), p. 83. Hereafter cited in text.

end attack them the more savagely. Wolfe begins his wry consideration of a person who forces us to examine our notions of the limits and definitions of the natural and the human with a snapshot of bleak, starved nature. This ambiguous image of the puny tree clearly represents whatever natural exists in this part of Carol Doda's world: Someone cares enough about preserving a bit of nature to have placed a metal sleeve around the base of its trunk to protect it from dog urine, but that artifact around the base of this starved, pathetic exemplar of nature only emphasizes how little of the natural still exists—and that it is losing the battle for survival—in this world. As Wolfe makes us recognize by the close of "The Put-Together Girl," nature, which Doda has tried to reject, cannot protect her and threatens its revenges upon her.

After thus presenting to us an emblematic picture of Carol Doda and her surroundings, Wolfe begins to explain what she has done, why she has done it, what benefits she has received, and what they have cost her—all of which facts together reveal her as someone representative of the modern world and hence as a warning about its dangers. He follows his initial mention of *them*, her breasts, by cataloguing the adverse effects they have had upon her life: Old Italian women walk by and call her a witch because of *them*, other women accuse her of being a prostitute because of *them*, and "grown men wearing rep ties and just emerging from long . . . liquid lunches walk by her and grin and aim their fingers at her like needles or guns or something and say, 'Pop! Pop!'—because of *them*" (84). Even she has begun to think of her artificially enlarged breasts as if they are not a part of her but possessions, things she has acquired that now dominate her existence. They provide her with a living and notoriety, if not fame, but they become the major fact in her relationships with other people, men or women. They have cost her the old easy-going relationship she used to have with her audience when she was just a dancer at the Condor. She can no longer walk in the street or even sleep normally since lying on her stomach or side produces too much discomfort.

In return, she has become something of a celebrity—one of San Francisco's resources, mocks Wolfe—and she enjoys the fact that crowds line up outside the nightclub to see her. Every night, seven nights a week, she dances standing on a piano as it is lowered to an eagerly awaiting audience, and although she is virtually nude, almost no one notices that fact, they are so eagerly craning their heads and waiting for *them*. When the piano finally descends, the audience sees the perfect Put-Together Girl, a parodic embodiment of all American tendencies *to make something of oneself.*

> The piano settles down, Carol Doda is on top of it dancing the Swim, the Jerk, the Frug, the Jump, the Spasm, the—her face is up above there like a pure white mask, an Easter Egg yellow explosion of hair on top, a pair of eyes with lashes like two sets of military shoe brushes, ice-white lips, two arms writhing around, her whole ilial complex writhing around, but all just a sort of pinwheel rosette for *them*. Carol Doda's breasts are up there the way one imagines Electra's should have been, two incredible mammiform protrusions, no mere pliable mass of feminine tissues and fats there but living arterial sculpture—viscera spigot—great blown-up aureate morning-glories. (85)

Wolfe's description, which makes his repugnance clear, emphasizes that good old-fashioned animal sexuality has been neither the goal nor the result of Doda's silicone injections. However wrong, however unnatural we might find her transformation, it relates only distantly to sexuality and sexual pleasure. Indeed, her entire performance, nudity and all, contains little of the conventional striptease and remains conspicuously unerotic. As Wolfe points out, "it is not a strip tease, it is no kind of *tease*, it is an animated cartoon, like the old Tom & Jerry cartoons where Tom, the cat, sees the bulldog coming and about forty-four sets of round white eyes—*boing*—go springing out of his eye sockets." Her routine has none of the bumps and grinds of the old-time burlesque house, and she seems absolutely unconscious of sexuality as she unsmilingly dances "like any little high school bud from the garden apartment next door at the Saturday-night dance bumping away doing the Monkey under a strawberry Feather Duster coiffure while her mother looks on from the side with a pleasant smile on her face as if to say, Well, yes, Carmen

109

is very social" (86). As Wolfe's sardonic analogy makes clear, he sees Carol Doda as typically American and typically modern in her conventional, unerotic use of the erotic.

In revealing the short distance that separates the high school bud, an ordinary adolescent, from this Put-Together Girl, Wolfe in Carlylean fashion provides a voice for contemporary phenomena, and like Carlyle, he invents an unidentified representative speaker. This voice tells us that Carol Doda's doctor has a long waiting list of women, "not showgirls," who want silicone injections: "Well, why," the voice asks, "should any woman *wait*—wait for what?—when the difference between dreariness and *appeal* is just a few centimeters of solid tissue here, a line stretched out there, a little body packing in the old thigh, under the wattles there—or perfect breasts? The philosophy of 'You have only one life to live, why not live it as a blonde?'—that is merely the *given*" (89). Claiming that even "conservative" New York hardly has left any older women with undyed hair, this California voice asks why people still speak of "'the natural order'? Such an old European idea—one means, well, the *wheel* violated the natural order, for god's sake; hot and cold running water violated it; wall ovens, spice bars, Reddi-Tap keg beer and Diz-Pos-Alls fracture the natural order—what are a few cubic centimeters of silicone?" (89–90). A possible invitation to a visit by deformity or death, it turns out, says Wolfe, but the voice takes no account of such dangers.

This voice, which defends silicone injections as the typical action of a typical American woman, in one sense is the idealized voice and consciousness of Doda herself, but I believe it is better understood as the voice of Modern America, which elevates artificiality above the natural without recognizing its cost. What makes Wolfe's parodic defense of such extensions of technology into our lives devastatingly effective is that he so thoroughly captures all the usual arguments for self-improvement. But what makes it resonate so disturbingly is that however much its colloquialisms and slovenly thinking undercut this defense, it embodies the fundamental assumptions, albeit in vulgarized form, of America and indeed all modern Western industrial democracies. We have the assumption, prevalent in advanced thought since

110

the French Revolution, that nature and the natural set no limits for human beings—only evil societies do that—and therefore we can be anything we wish. The modern faith in technology, which implements such assumptions, has produced antibiotics and wall ovens, modern sanitation and silicone-injected breasts. And although we might be tempted to respond that Wolfe's voice of the age has made a basic error by thus glibly claiming that the wheel, plumbing, and silicone-enhanced breasts are all technological improvements that violate natural order, we find distinguishing among them on these grounds difficult, and Wolfe does not assist us. [18]

Although he does not help us answer these crucial questions about where the proper limits between nature and technological artifice lie, he does, in the manner of the sage, reveal further meaning in "The Put-Together Girl." First, Wolfe makes clear that the germ of this particular technological distortion of the human body lies in male attitudes toward women's bodies. Second, he shows that women's willingness to conform to men's attitudes arises, not out of sexual needs, but out of the universal need to acquire stature for oneself. After having the voice defend silicone injections as just another example of modern technological improvement, Wolfe includes a paragraph of straightforward exposition that sets forth some of the obvious physical dangers of these injections, and he points out that women in California and Nevada are nonetheless willing to risk cancer or other as yet unknown illnesses themselves, and they are also willing to risk the health of their teenage daughters "because they

---

[18]This basic criticism of all technology has a venerable history in American literature. Emerson, we recall, argued in the chapter "Wealth" in *English Traits*: "The machine unmans the user. What he gains in making cloth, he loses in general power. There should be temperance in making cloth, as well as in eating. A man should not be a silk-worm; nor a nation a tent of caterpillars. The robust rural Saxon degenerates in the mills into the Leicester stockinger, to the imbecile Manchester spinner,—far on the way to be spiders and needles. The incessant repetition of the same hand-work dwarfs the man, robs him of his strength, wit, and versatility, to make a pin-polisher, a buckle-maker, or any other speciality; and presently, in a change of industry, whole towns are sacrificed like ant-hills, when the fashion of shoe-strings supersedes buckles, when cotton takes the place of linen, or railways of turnpikes, or when commons are enclosed by the landlords" (857).

111

aren't developing fast enough to . . . compete; well, Carmen *is* social. And actually it's such a simple thing in a man's world where men have such simple ideas" (90; ellipsis in original). Carol Doda, then, exists in Tom Wolfe's essay as a symptom and a warning—a Sign of the Times—of modern man's pathetic attempts to create importance for himself in the absence of natural and other standards. The specific occasion of the warning is a young woman who has had her breasts enlarged with injections of a silicone compound to make something of herself, and like so many of us, implies Wolfe, she has made something artificial and unnatural of herself. She embodies the dangers of modern technology, the absurd relations between men and women, and the results of a universal drive for status and significance, one that Wolfe apparently finds more influential in a well-fed modern society than those of hunger or sexuality.

Like Carlyle, Wolfe takes apparently trival contemporary phenomena as his subject and reveals that they provide unexpected ways into a nation's state of mind and soul. Furthermore, like the orthodox sage, he expends considerable energy mocking contemporary destructions of language and explaining what some key words mean, though often from his subject's and not his own point of view. As we shall see in chapter 4, he also acts like those sages who purport to be Masters of Experience, promising to give accounts of phenomena from the inside and thus providing experiential truths otherwise unobtainable to us. At the same time, he is an expert at creating credibility for the seer's voice that dominates his many excursions into the weird and wacky world of the sixties and seventies. Nonetheless, in "The Put-Together Girl" and similar writings Wolfe is not writing as a sage in the manner of Carlyle and Thoreau because his works lack two chief requirements of the genre: Writing as a brilliant satirist, he has no positive program and no final, solacing vision; and furthermore, because he does not have such a positive program, he does not employ the full prophetic pattern. His brilliantly mordant pieces begin by picking up some bit of grotesque contemporary trivia which he then interprets, and although his interpretations contain implicit judgments and warnings for his audience, he neither attacks it directly nor offers a closing visionary prom-

112

ise. Such modifications, extensions, and attenuations of a literary form always mark the later stages of genre development.

If Wolfe's represents one possible modern extension or intonation of the genre of the sage, Germaine Greer's use of grotesque technological manipulation of the human body exemplifies how work in other forms of nonfiction can employ symbolical grotesques. At the close of her discussion in *The Female Eunuch* of the sexual stereotypes that confine women, Greer tells the tale of April Ashley, who was born male but so longed to become a woman that he had an operation to change his sex. "He wanted," she adds, "soft fabrics, jewels, furs, makeup, the love and protection of men"—all those things women typically desire, according to the stereotype. Impotent and not attracted to women, he also did not "particularly welcome homosexual addresses. He did not think of himself as a pervert, or even as a transvestite, but as a woman cruelly transmogrified into manhood."[19] He finally found a doctor in Casablanca who proposed a solution acceptable to Ashley: He would remake him into a woman, or something very like a woman, slicing away the unnecessary apparatus and re-engineering it into something more desired. "He was to be castrated, and his penis used as the lining of a surgically constructed cleft, which would be a vagina. He would be infertile, but that has never affected the attribution of femininity." After hormone treatments had removed his beard and produced tiny breasts, April returned to England, "became a model, and began to illustrate the feminine stereotype as he was perfectly qualified to do, for he was elegant, voluptuous, beautifully groomed, and in love with his own image." Unfortunately for him (her?), April made the mistake of marrying an heir to a peerage, thus "acting out the highest achievement of the feminine dream, and went to live with him in a villa in Marbella." The marriage was never consummated, and Justice Omerod ruled that April remained in law a member of the male sex. About this failed attempt to make something of oneself, Greer concludes that April's sexual incompetence as a woman is to be expected from a castrated male,

---

[19]*The Female Eunuch* (New York, McGraw-Hill, 1971), p. 54. All succeeding quotations from Greer's discussion of Ashley come from this and the following page.

but in fact it does not differ from the impotence of stereotypically "feminine women," who endure sexual relations without experiencing sexual desire. As long, says Greer, as the feminine stereotype "remains the definition of the female sex, April Ashley is a woman, regardless of the legal decision ensuing from her divorce. She is as much a casualty of the sexes as we all are. Disgraced, unsexed April Ashley is our sister and our symbol." Like the Victorian sage, Greer has taken a contemporary phenomenon, in this case an identifiable person, and by looking closely at this person, she has transformed him into a grotesque emblem of woman, a sexual Sign of the Times.

Similarities obviously exist between Greer's treatment of April Ashley and Wolfe's treatment of Carol Doda: Both take as the object of interpretation living human bodies that physicians, using the latest technology, have modified to attract men. Both writers make clear that although these technological reconstructions have made female celebrities of the people involved, the knife and the needle failed to create true sexuality; technology can parody, not create, the natural. Although both authors present suitably chilling descriptions of the procedures involved, they concentrate instead upon the meanings implicit in having chosen to undergo such changes and deformations. Both Greer and Wolfe, in other words, present a person as a grotesque Sign of the Times, an incarnation of the sickness of the age. Both authors emphasize that society dehumanizes women's bodies, and both derive this dehumanization at least in part from the power that men hold over women. Both, finally, employ their satirical grotesques as a means of discussing the nature of power and status in modern life.

Nonetheless, despite the fact that they have many of the same ideas and emphases, they use this technique of the sage for somewhat different literary purposes. Wolfe employs his symbolical grotesque as the stylistic and formal center of "The Put-Together Girl"—it essentially generates his entire essay—whereas Greer uses hers, much as Ruskin often does, to provide a set piece that sums up and extends all the ideas of a chapter. Furthermore, although one can justifiably categorize Wolfe's "Put-Together Girl" and similar essays as new or extended versions of the genre of the sage, one cannot do the same with *The Female Eunuch*, a work that exemplifies the ways individual devices of this genre have become common property in recent nonfiction. I must emphasize that when I claim one work belongs to the genre of the sage and another does not, I am not making judgments concerning their literary value or even their polemical effectiveness. In fact, in the case of Greer's and Wolfe's Put-Together Girls, I have chosen examples that both work equally well, though in quite different literary and ideological settings. If my hypothesis that defining such a genre makes for better reading of nonfiction proves correct, then I hope it would follow that one can cast light on related literary forms, including the novel, by showing how the sage has made particular techniques popular and available.

3

The Word Restored:
Definition, Redefinition,
and Satiric Redefinition

The Sage's Definitions

Another chief device of the sage, one common to all forms of argumentation, is definition. By providing the meaning of terms crucial to one's discourse, one obviously moves that discourse in directions one can control. Moreover, such acts of definition implicitly assert that the audience, whether listeners or readers, depends entirely upon the sage—for without the sage, the person who knows the true meaning of things, members of the audience ostensibly cannot even communicate, either with one another or with reality. The essence of such a far-reaching claim lies in the fact that the sage (or someone else who uses such techniques of definition) purports to know as others do not the true relation of language to reality. Just as the sage's moral stature derives from the fact that he knows the good and his audience has lost sight of it, so too his intellectual stature here comes from the asserted fact that he alone can use language correctly. In fact, the sage implicitly—and sometimes explicitly—maintains that he, and he alone, can restore language to its supposedly pristine efficiency and authenticity.

Both these claims and the moral emphasis with which they are generally made derive from the homiletic tradition. Victorian preachers like Charles Kingsley emphasized that in religious matters the believer had a moral duty to get language right and use words correctly. Thus, in differentiating between religion and godliness in a sermon on that subject, Kingsley earnestly instructs his listeners that "a difference in words is a very awful, important difference." He does so in part to make the preacher's usual claim to understand the correct meaning of essential words—and his further claim to restore true meaning to such words and thereby place his audience once again in a proper, healthy, vital relationship to reality. Kingsley therefore assures his listeners:

> A difference in words is a difference in things. Words are very awful and wonderful things, for they come from the most awful and wonderful of all beings, Jesus Christ, the Word. He puts words into men's minds. He made all things, and He makes all words to express those things with. And woe to those who use the wrong words about things! For if a man calls anything by its wrong name, it is a sure sign that he understands that thing wrongly, or feels about it wrongly; and therefore a man's words are often honester than he thinks; for as a man's words are, so is a man's heart . . . and, therefore, by right words, by the right names which we call things, we shall be justified, and by our words, by the wrong names we call things, we shall be condemned.[1]

Furthermore, Kingsley also sounds a familiar theme of the sages when he emphasizes in "The Spirit and the Flesh" that "according to a nation's godliness, and wisdom, and purity of heart, will be its power of using words discreetly and reverently" (43). Placing such importance upon the ability to use language correctly, Kingsley as preacher expectedly opens many sermons with questions of definition. For example, he begins

---

[1]"Religion not Godliness," *Village Sermons, and Town and Country Sermons* (London, Macmillan, 1886), pp. 11–12. Hereafter cited in text.

117

"Self-Destruction," a sermon on 1 Kings 22:23, by directing the audience's attention to the way in which the appointed text provides "an insight into the meaning of that most awful and terrible word,—temptation" (59), and he begins "The Courage of the Saviour," a sermon on John 11:7–8, by defining *fortitude* (184–85).

Carlyle employs the preacher's emphasis upon definition for an appropriate subject in *Past and Present*. The "Gospel of Mammonism" asks the reader if he knows the meaning of the words *heaven* and *hell*. "I rather apprehend, not. Often as the words are on our tongue, they have got a fabulous or semi-fabulous character for most of us. . . . Yet it is well worth while for us to know, once and always, that they are not a similitude, nor a fable nor a semi-fable; that they are an everlasting highest fact!" (10.144–45). Citing as authority Sauertieg, a character he created in *Sartor Resartus*, Carlyle first quotes his remarks that although the English use the word *hell* frequently, they do so with such lack of clarity that one cannot "ascertain what they meant by it," after which, speaking through the mask of Sauertieg, he argues by means of a series of definitions.

> Hell generally signifies the Infinite Terror, the thing a man *is* infinitely afraid of, and shudders and shrinks from, struggling with his whole soul to escape from it. There is a Hell therefore, if you will consider, which accompanies man, in all stages of his history, and religious or other development: but the Hells of men and Peoples differ notably. With Christians it is the infinite terror of being found guilty before the Just Judge. With old Romans, I conjecture, it was the terror not of Pluto, for whom they probably cared little, but of doing unworthily, doing unvirtuously, which was their word for unmanfully. And now what is it, if you pierce through his Cants, his oft-repeated Hearsays, what he calls his Worships and so forth,—what is it that the modern English soul does, in very truth, dread infinitely, and contemplate with entire despair? What *is* his Hell, after all these reputable, oft-repeated Hearsays, what is it? With hesitation, with astonishment, I pronounce it to be the terror of "Not succeeding"; of not making money, fame, or some other figure in the world,—chiefly of not making money! (10.145–46)

This kind of hell, he decides, "belongs naturally to the Gospel of Mammonism, which has also its corresponding Heaven.... About one thing we are entirely in earnest: The making of money" (10.146). Carlyle, who denies the importance of belief in a hell as a literal place, here writes about the kind of issues discussed by the preacher and takes the preacher's attitude toward a congregation.

Carlyle's explanation of what *hell* means to his contemporaries exemplifies the pattern of the sage's definitions. The sage's acts of definition take three basic forms—definition, corrective redefinition, and satiric definition. Ruskin's definitions of *imitation, truth, beauty, imagination, theoria,* and *composition* in *Modern Painters* and *wealth* and *value* in *Unto This Last* exemplify simple definition, the most basic form of this technique and that kind found in all types of discourse. His definitions of *imitation* and *truth*, which play an important part in his polemical defense of Turner and nineteenth-century painters of landscape, have little explicitly polemical about them, and this is because Ruskin wishes both to set forth the theoretical bases of his defense of the new art and also to convince his reader that, however much a polemicist he may appear at times, his argument derives from the most rational premises. Perhaps the most important of these premises is that the visual arts chiefly involve statements of truth rather than of imitation. According to the chapter "Of Ideas of Imitation," Fuseli, Burke, and Coleridge falsely distinguished between imitation and copying, both of which produce a rather low and limited, but nonetheless authentic, form of pleasure, for "whenever anything looks like what it is not, the resemblance being so great as *nearly* to deceive, we feel a kind of pleasurable surprise, an agreeable excitement of mind, exactly the same in its nature as we receive from juggling. Whenever we perceive this in something produced by art, that is to say, whenever the work is seen to resemble something which we know it is not, we receive what I call an idea of imitation" (3.100). Although he admits that imitation, which earlier critics had made the central principle of the arts, does produce a genuine source of aesthetic pleasure, he argues that it is but a comparatively minor one; for art proceeds by statements about form, rather than by imitations

119

of it. For example, a marble statue of a man, says Ruskin, is not an imitation of a human being but the actual form of one. "Form is form, *bonâ fide* and actual, whether in marble or in flesh—not an imitation or resemblance of form, but real form. The chalk outline of the bough of a tree on paper, is not an imitation; it looks like chalk and paper—not like wood, and that which it suggests to the mind is not properly said to be *like* the form of a bough, it *is* the form of a bough" (3.101). Ideas of truth, rather than ideas of imitation, therefore, provide the central pleasures of visual art; and "the word Truth, as applied to art, signifies the faithful statement, either to the mind or senses, of any fact of nature. We receive an idea of truth, then, when we perceive the faithfulness of such a statement" (3.104).

The second technique at which we shall look, that of denying the validity of an accepted definition or common application of one, takes a purely negative form. As Thoreau's "A Plea for Captain John Brown" shows, one particularly aggressive, effective way that the sage can show his audience that it misunderstands and misuses language is by directly contradicting common usage. In his defense of the great abolitionist, he thus attacks the way his contemporaries have labeled John Brown insane: "Insane! A father and six sons, and one son-in-law, and several more men besides,—as many at least as twelve disciples,—all struck with insanity at once; while the sane tyrant holds with a firmer gripe than ever his four millions of slaves, and a thousand sane editors, his abettors, are saving their country and their bacon" (126). By the time Thoreau completes this sentence, he has shown that his countrymen, who have committed themselves to live by the principle of expediency rather than those of truth, religion, and justice, misapply the word *insane*. After first suggesting how improbable such a simultaneous attack of madness would have been, he makes clear that, in a society which allows slavery, sanity is equivalent to evil and expedience. The tyrant is sane, and a thousand newspaper editors support the enslavement of other human beings in order to protect their own means of gaining a living. These editors, Thoreau implies, corrupt the language for financial gain.[2] At this point in his attack

[2] In "Slavery in Massachusetts" Thoreau had earlier attacked contemporary

upon his contemporaries' use of the words *sane* and *insane*, he points to the fact that his northern neighbors did not judge Brown's successful efforts in Kansas to be insane, and he directs his audience to ask the tyrant, who is his most dangerous foe—the sane or the insane man? Finally, he inquires: "Do the thousands who know him best, who have rejoiced at his deeds in Kansas, and have afforded him material aid there, think him insane? Such a use of this word is a mere trope with most who persist in using it, and I have no doubt that many of the rest have already in silence retracted their words" (126). Thoreau's various ways of using this device of attacking a commonplace definition reveal how he makes it the focus of the entire passage. This technique, which gathers others to it, emphasizes both the intellectual and moral weakness of the position he opposes.

Then, when he compares the "manly directness and force" of Brown's words on being captured at Harper's Ferry to the speeches of the members of Congress from Massachusetts and other northern states, Thoreau makes explicit the point at the heart of his strategy: Correct use of language, true language, can appear only in the mouths of the good, for moral and political corruption corrupts language and its users. Brown, therefore, speaks an authentic language: "Truth is his inspirer, and earnestness the polisher of his sentences. He could afford to lose his Sharps' rifles, while he retained his faculty of speech, a Sharps' rifle of infinitely surer and longer range" (127).

Matthew Arnold's famous definition of *culture*, which also makes use of the same intertwined claims of intellectual and moral superiority, well exemplifies the next step or stage in this series of associated techniques: corrective redefinition. Whereas

---

journalism with fierce invective: "Could slavery suggest a more complete servility than some of these journals exhibit? Is there any dust which their conduct does not lick, and make fouler still with its slime? I do not know whether the Boston *Herald* is still in existence, but I remember to have seen it about the streets when Simms was carried off.... When I have taken up this paper with my cuffs turned up, I have heard the gurgling of the sewer through every column. I have felt that I was handling a paper picked out of the public gutters, a leaf from the gospel of the gambling-house, the groggery and the brothel, harmonizing with the gospel of the Merchants' Exchange" (101).

121

Thoreau's attack upon the application of the word *insane* to Brown and his followers is a purely negative technique, used only for purposes of attack, corrective definition (or redefinition) follows an initial attack upon received meaning by the sage's assertion of a correct one. Like the sage's use of the prophetic pattern, corrective definition follows negative by positive. For example, at the opening of *Culture and Anarchy*, Arnold directly confronts opposing points of view, which are in fact opposing interpretations, by claiming that his opponents do not in fact understand the words they use. According to him, "the disparagers of culture make its motive curiosity; sometimes, indeed, they make its motive mere exclusiveness and vanity." These latter opponents of culture claim that "it is valued either out of sheer vanity and ignorance or else as an engine of social and class distinction, separating its holder, like a badge or title, from other people who have not got it." Like Ruskin, Arnold well knew the standard code words that had such appeal to many Evangelicals in his intended audience, and he uses one of them—*serious*—to advance his cause. Many raised as evangelicals both within and without the Church of England took rather puritanical attitudes toward secular culture because they believed the truly serious person, the person concerned with the things of Christ, did not have much time, energy, or attention for such essentially trivial activities. Confronting this source of opposition head on, Arnold uses a device particularly popular in the Evangelical sermon, claiming that those who thus interpret the meaning of the term *culture* both do not know the meaning of the word and also, by their misuse of it, demonstrate that they are not "serious" people: "No serious man would call this *culture*, or attach any value to it, as culture, at all" (5.90). As Arnold, who would have made a fine advertising copywriter, was well aware, his charge that his opponents were not "serious" bore with this suggestion of a basic lack of earnestness a subtle suggestion that such intellectual lightness and frivolity undoubtedly connected to an unenviable moral and spiritual state.[3] Then, having first turned the tables upon his

---

[3]Geoffrey Tillotson rather savagely describes this side of him in "Matthew Arnold: The Critic and the Advocate," in *Critics and Criticism in the Nineteenth Century* (London, Athlone Press, 1951), pp. 52–53: "We can see Arnold as a

self-righteous opponents by appropriating one of their favorite cant terms, Arnold again turns the tables on them when he argues that he and all other lovers of culture are the truly "serious" men, for according to him, culture implies both the "desire to see things as they are" and a corollary "balance and regulation of mind." Culture, he adds, is "properly described" as deriving from "the love of perfection; it is a *study of perfection*. It moves by the force, not merely or primarily of the scientific passion for pure knowledge, but also of the moral and social passion for doing good" (5.91). Culture, in other words, hardly implies, as its opponents had charged, either idle curiosity or exclusiveness and vanity. Rather culture turns out to be, in contrast, an essentially moral and religious matter—a matter, in fact, of particularly high seriousness, a matter to engage the minds and souls of all truly "serious" men and women.[4]

The third kind of definition, the satirical, does not mock some particular received meaning but uses definition as part of a satiric attack upon something else. In "A Plea for Captain John Brown," Thoreau makes a characteristically aggressive use of satirical definition to provide a climax to his attack on those who will not resist slavery. His satiric definition first charges contemporary Christians with ignoring any aspect of their faith that might force them to undertake difficult acts: "The modern Christian is a man who has consented to say all the prayers in the liturgy, provided you will let him go straight to bed and sleep qui-

---

clever salesman, a 'portly jeweller from Cheapside', a Bottles as clever as any of those he sought to charm into hearing him. We can see him creating the demand for those particular goods of which he held stock.... If they bought—and buy many of them did—they bought because they had been got at by a salesman as expert as themselves. For Arnold drew on all the machinery of salesmanship to carry through his great deal. He was a great selling 'personality', the Shaw of his age; and, as Mr. Garrod has seen, what were the constantly recurring phrases—'grand style', 'high seriousness', 'primary human emotions', 'sweetness and light'—what were they but the slogans that undermined resistance to sales?" See also pp. 66–67.

[4]Removed from the context of the passage in which it appears, Arnold's definition of culture might appear to exemplify the simplest, most basic form of this technique. But the preceding statements that prepare for it and the tone with which Arnold presents his conception of culture transform it into an instance of aggressively corrective introduction.

etly afterward. All his prayers begin with 'Now I lay me down to sleep'." Although willing after a fashion to perform certain long-established charities, he "does not wish to hear of any new-fangled ones; he doesn't wish to have any supplementary articles added to the contract, to fit it to the present time." Like Ruskin who charges in "Traffic" that the contemporary Christian is a Christian only in church, Thoreau mocks him for showing the "whites of his eyes on the Sabbath, and the blacks all the rest of the week" (121).[5] Thoreau in fact occasionally holds that any established faith must be an inauthentic, purely nominal one in the nineteenth century: "Really, there is no infidelity, now-a-days, so great as that which prays, and keeps the Sabbath, and rebuilds the churches.... The church is a sort of hospital for men's souls, and as full of quackery as the hospital for their bodies. Those who are taken into it live like pensioners in their Retreat or Sailor's Snug Harbor, where you may see a row of religious cripples sitting outside in sunny weather."[6]

A somewhat different form of satiric definition appears in "Slavery in Massachusetts," which uses a fairly straightforward examination of the meaning of the word *governor* to set in motion a series of contrasts between ideal and actual, theory and practice. In particular, this prophetic attack upon contemporary iniquity contrasts what a governor of Massachusetts is supposed to do—enforce all the laws, including those that protect everyone in the state—with the present governor's failure to perform these duties by permitting someone living in the state to be returned to southern slavery. This examination of the term *governor* is part of Thoreau's main or underlying point that the seizure of a single person of another race is not only relevant to the lives of

[5]Emerson, who makes a less topical and hence less savage application of this topos, points out in his "Lecture on the Times" that his contemporaries separate religion and life: "Religion was not invited to eat or drink or sleep with us, or to make or divide an estate, but was a holiday guest. Such omissions judge the church" (161). Emerson, like many others, extends this distinction from religion to other matters when he argues in "The Young American" that if we must have kings and nobles, since "Nature provides such in every society,—only let us have the real instead of the titular" (225).

[6]*A Week on the Concord and Merrimack Rivers*, ed. Carl F. Hovde et al. (Princeton, Princeton University Press, 1980), p. 76.

every member of his audience but centrally so since the act directly limits and threatens their own freedom. This exercise in definition produces a second implication as well: Since the governor, the chief executive officer of Massachusetts, did not guard the rights of one who lived in his domain, he has therefore proved himself not to be a governor at all, and therefore, Thoreau implies, he has forfeited the obedience due one.

Thoreau begins his definition by taking the satirist's pose of the ingenuous novice—the honorable, childlike idealist who believes all he is told. "I had thought that the Governor was in some sense the executive officer of the State; that it was his business, as a Governor, to see that the laws of the State were executed; while, as a man, he took care that he did not, by so doing, break the laws of humanity. . . . Perhaps I do not know what are the duties of a Governor; but if to be a Governor requires to subject oneself to such much ignominy without remedy, if it is to put a restraint upon my manhood, I shall take care never to be Governor of Massachusetts" (94). Much in the manner of Evangelical ministers and writers of tracts, he thus proceeds by claiming that the governor is a false governor, not a true one—a governor in name only, not in act. Thoreau relates that when he searches for a governor, he only finds an empty simulacrum, a shell, a pageant-governor:

> I listen to hear the voice of a Governor, Commander-in-Chief of the forces of Massachusetts. I hear only the creaking of crickets and the hum of insects which now fill the summer air. The Governor's exploit is to review the troops on muster days. I have seen him on horseback, with his hat off, listening to a chaplain's prayer. It chances that is all I have ever seen of a Governor. I think that I could manage to get along without one. If *he* is not of the least use to prevent my being kidnapped, pray of what important use is he likely to be to me? When freedom is most endangered, he dwells in the deepest obscurity. (92)

Even before pointing out that the governor who does not defend one's freedom does nothing, Thoreau implicitly defines him as one who does nothing while simultaneously mocking another group he takes to be respectable do-nothings: "A distinguished

125

clergyman told me that he chose the profession of a clergyman because, it afforded the most leisure for literary pursuits. I would recommend to him the profession of a Governor" (92–93). As these examples reveal, Thoreau combines straightforward acts of definition with those of a satirical nature. Having first stated the true meaning of a central term, he then mocks those who have not lived up to it. The implication of such a manner of proceeding is, once again, that the speaker, the definer of important terms, resides at the center of meaning. He alone knows what things mean. He also sees clearly enough to warn others that they have fallen away from the ways of God and nature. To find that way, claims Thoreau the sage, his audience must first understand the true meaning of words, and therefore he begins with the word *governor* and follows this definition with others, such as *slavery*, which are even more central to his argument. By the time that Thoreau has finished attacking the governor of Massachusetts with this satirically employed definition, he has transformed him, his office, and the element of sham they share into a grotesque metonymy of his age and nation.

Thoreau's entire strategy here seems to derive from Carlyle's *French Revolution*, which explains that central phenomenon of modern history as the necessary purgation of government that does not govern. This thematized technique of contrasting definition and actions that fail to match it derives in turn from the common Evangelical Protestant distinction between *practical* (or *practicing*) and *nominal* religion spread by William Wilberforce's enormously popular devotional work *A Practical View of the Prevailing System of Professed Christians, in the Higher and Middle Classes in this Country, Contrasted with Real Christianity* (1819), commonly known as *Practical Christianity*. The Victorian sages use the distinction between practical and nominal religious, moral, and political belief for powerfully satiric effects. For example, in "Traffic," after Ruskin has instructed his audience that a nation's architecture inevitably expresses its basic attitudes and beliefs, he explains those implicit in Greek, medieval, and renaissance styles and then asks, "Will you tell me what *we* worship, and what *we* build? You know," he confides to his audience, "we are speaking always of the real, active, continual national worship; that by which men act, while they live; not that which they talk of, when they die" (18.447). According to Ruskin, "we have, indeed, a nominal religion, to which we pay tithes of property and sevenths of time; but we have also a practical and earnest religion, to which we devote nine-tenths of our property, and six-sevenths of our time. And we dispute a great deal about the nominal religion: but we are all unanimous about this practical one; of which I think you will admit that the ruling goddess may be best generally described as the 'Goddess of Getting-on', or 'Britannia of the Market'" (18.447–48). When Ruskin thus defines the religious faith of his Midlands audience, emphasizing that he seeks an essential, not superficial, meaning of the term, he obviously follows William Wilberforce's method, one with which his audience would have been very familiar.[7]

Definition as Theme and Technique

In definition, as in other techniques of this literary mode, theme and technique, form and content often inextricably intertwine. For example, the central role of definition in the works of nineteenth- and twentieth-century sages implies that only the speaker knows the true meaning of words, that the audience has lost knowledge both of the words its members use and of the reality to which these words refer, and that, finally, only the sage still retains the capacity for true speech. Just as Thoreau's destructive definition of *governor* inevitably blends definition, satire, elaborate emblems, interpretation, prophetic diagnosis of his society's essential problems, and prognosis of a coming spiritual disaster—in short, virtually all the elements that make up

---

[7]Thoreau, like Emerson, employs this distinction between real and nominal, which he applies to political affairs, in the form of the "What is called . . ." *topos:* "What is called politics is comparatively something so superficial and inhuman, that, practically, I have never fairly recognized that it concerns me at all. The newspapers, I perceive, devote some of their columns specially to politics or government without charge; and this, one would say, is all that saves it; but, as I love literature, and, to some extent, the truth also, I never read those columns at any rate. I do not wish to blunt my sense of right so much. I have not got to answer for having read a single President's Message" (177).

the genre of the sage—so too definition as technique naturally, inevitably, merges with definition as theme.

The assumption implicit in the sage's more aggressive uses of definition—namely, that as a society falls away from the ways of God and nature, its language degenerates—frequently becomes an explicit theme, particularly in the works of twentieth-century practitioners of the genre. Arnold, who begins *Culture and Anarchy* with a corrective definition, sees such degeneration as both cause and symptom of Victorian England's disastrous lack of mental cultivation. Part of the problem, he finds, lies in the fact that "candidates for political influence and leadership, who thus caress the self-love of those whose suffrages they desire, . . . are using a sort of conventional language, or what we call clap-trap" (5.152). Whatever they diagnose as the ultimate cause, all nineteenth- and twentieth-century sages find such claptrap to be a Sign of the Times. As Joan Didion puts it in *Slouching towards Bethlehem*: "The center was not holding. It was a country of bankruptcy notices and public-auction announcements and commonplace reports of casual killings and misplaced children and abandoned homes and vandals who misspelled even the four-letter words they scrawled" (84). Even the well-meaning hippies and radicals, she argues, have no command of language, no words to use: "Because they do not believe in words—words are for 'typeheads' . . . and a thought which needs words is just one more of those ego trips—their only proficient vocabulary is in the society's platitudes. As it happens I am still committed to the idea that the ability to think for oneself depends upon one's mastery of the language, and I am not optimistic about children who will settle for saying, to indicate that their mother and father do not live together, that they come from 'a broken home'" (123).

Like many writers since Carlyle and the German romantics, Mailer believes technology in some way to blame for such pervasive claptrap. *Of a Fire on the Moon* presents as related struggles his battle to find an adequate language, a language adequate to idea and experience, and that to interpret the meaning and value of the entire moon project. His problem as a writer, whether as mere reporter or sage, is that "the language which now would sing of this extraordinary vault promised to be as flat as an unstrung harp. The century had unstrung any melody of words" (130).[8] Throughout the early portions of the book, when he tries to get his bearings, he repeatedly comes upon the problems posed for the interpreter by technological language, and although he early confesses his admiration for the astronauts and envy for their opportunity, he finds himself troubled by their use of a peculiarly deadened, peculiarly twentieth-century form of language which insulates reality from speaker and hearer. "Even as the Nazis and the Communists had used to speak of mass murder as liquidation, so the astronauts spoke of possible personal disasters as 'contingency.' The heart of astronaut talk, like the heart of all bureaucratic talk, was a jargon which could be easily converted to computer programming, a language like Fortran or Cobol or Algol." According to Mailer, "Anti-dread formulations were the center of it, as if words like pills were there to suppress emotional symptoms" (25). But for him language should bring one closer to reality, make one more alive to it, and therefore such formulaic, impersonal, often inaccurate speech kills the human and the humane in each of us. Mailer, always sensitive to language, heaps up a series of examples of such deadspeak. One of the astronauts, responding no to a reporter's question, says:

"that's not a prerogative we have available to us." He could of course have said, "We can't do it," but in trouble he always talked computerese. The use of "we" was discouraged. "A joint exercise has demonstrated" became the substitution. "Other choices" became "peripheral secondary objectives." "Doing our best" was "obtaining maximum advantage possible." "Confidence" became "very high confidence level." . . . The message had to be locked

[8]As Mailer explains, "One of the cess-filled horrors of the Twentieth Century slowly seeping in on the journalists was that they were becoming obsolete. Events were developing in a style and structure that made them almost impossible to write about. . . . A process was taking place that was too complex to be reported for daily news stories by passing observers, and so the process itself began to produce the news for the reporters. Their work had come down to rewriting publicity handouts" (88).

129

into a form which could be transmitted by pulse or lack of pulse, one binary digit at a time, one bit, one bug to be installed in each box. You could not break through computerese. (39)

Although Mailer remains fully aware of the practical justifications of such a narcotizing language that thus assiduously omits all human elements, he also perceives at what cost it protects the speaker and listener from worrisome possibilities.

One of the most terrifying consequences of such deadening language appears to him when he encounters the sublimities of the space ship within a mammoth structure, the world's largest, and then perceives that the men who can create such incredible machines no longer possess the language to make others understand what they have done. Indeed, the names they choose for their creations always produce bathos. Having found himself moved by the immense size of the space ship and then recognizing, in something like a religious conversion, that the future has arrived, Mailer wonders:

> Yet all the signs leading to the Vehicle Assembly Building said VAB. VAB—it could be the name of a drink or a deodorant, or it could be suds for the washer. But it was not a name for this warehouse of the gods. The great churches of a religious age had names: the Alhambra, Santa Sophia, Mont-Saint-Michel, Chartres, Westminster Abbey, Notre Dame. Now: VAB. Nothing fit anything any longer. The art of communication had become the mechanical function, and the machine was the work of art. What a fall for the ego of the artist. What a climb to capture the language again! (55–56)

Here Mailer brings together many of his central concerns throughout this volume. To begin with, he points out that a new practical, practicing religion, as Ruskin and Carlyle put it, is in the works, and its monuments are not cathedrals but gigantic creations of modern technology. These changes represent fundamental shifts in the nature of man and society that puzzle one—and demand interpretation: They provide the interpretive cruxes, the material of the sage. Finally, much that demands interpretation concerns the essential problem of language, which appears to have become corrupted, or at least so changed that it no longer connects us with reality.

Although the technique of definition appears in all forms of argumentation, it plays a particularly important role in the writings of the sage, in part because it blends so effectively with his other approaches, such as attacks upon the audience, and in part because it provides a ready means of demonstrating the audience's need for the sage and his message. Such acts of definition imply that the audience, whether because of its own faults or because of those of others, lacks a language adequate to its needs. Above all, it lacks a language adequate to reality, and the sage's definitions imply that he has one and will share it.

4

The Sage as Master of Experience

In a manner somewhat similar to that by which sages present themselves as the masters and true possessors of language, some also present themselves as masters of experience. John Ruskin, D. H. Lawrence, Norman Mailer, Tom Wolfe, and other authors who purport to offer their readers the true experience of some event or phenomenon essentially lend them their own sensibilities, and by doing so such writers imply that they can provide information otherwise unavailable. Since the sage argues that his audience has fallen away from the true path, he occasionally demonstrates the cost to them of their fall by showing what they have failed to see or feel. In fact, he reveals to them that they have become deadened to the truth or beauty of reality, that they need someone to remove their blinders or educate their vision. Ruskin and other sages who present themselves as masters of visual and other experience also offer their own intense experiences of reality as a standard for their audiences and teach them the correct way to see, think, and feel. The sage teaches, in other words, how to approach reality correctly. Of course, in testing relevant experience upon his own pulse, as it were, the sage obviously presents himself as the one in charge, as the

132

single source of knowledge and wisdom. This manner of proceeding has several possible effects. First, it can thus simply offer readers some information they cannot otherwise obtain, but it can also emphasize that only the sage can provide it at all. Furthermore, the sage's self-presentation as master of experience can, like his particularly aggressive acts of definition, make clear that the audience has fallen away from the truth and desperately needs him to help them return. Thus, although this stance also serves to create credibility for the writer, it may have as well the far more polemical effect of attacking his opponents, audience, or both.

These emphases upon authentic experience and the writer's superior ability to obtain it point to the romantic roots of the genre. In the first place, unlike the wisdom statements of Joseph Addison or Samuel Johnson, such work not only avoids generalization, but also takes as its most obvious program the communication of specific facts. Second, not only does it side with romantic specificity in opposition to neoclassical generalization, but it also obviously takes the romantic position that truths of physical and mental experience, rather than the ideas we may generalize from them, are the proper way into understanding whatever subject may be under investigation.

G. Robert Stange is almost certainly correct when he argues that such attempts to communicate the feeling of a particular experience in nonfictional prose first appeared in nineteenth-century art criticism. According to him, whereas eighteenth-century prose had been primarily "cognitive, by the middle of the nineteenth century it had become expressionist," and in the work of what he terms "conscious prose stylists" from Lamb to Pater "logical organization and a conceptual framework are more and more often abandoned in favor of emotive effects and a perceptual scheme." In particular, as Stange points out, the writer "tends to avoid the abstract in favor of the immediate: he will try to imitate a speaking voice, or express the rhythm of the mind as it responds to or perceives concrete experience. Special value is attached to image sequences, to discrete data of precise observation," and to representing "particular aesthetic as well as emotional experiences."[1]

Word-painting, or the creation of visually composed passages of description, constitutes one of the sage's chief means of portraying a mind in the process of experiencing something. Such word-painting, particularly as employed by Ruskin and his followers, matches all Stange's descriptions of a new form of prose: Emphasizing a perceptual scheme, generally that of the moving eye, it conveys the immediate experience of discrete phenomena by means of image sequences, precise observation, and dramatized acts of perception. A major source of such Ruskinian word-painting, perhaps the only one of any significance, is Ann Radcliffe, whose novels first fully developed the technique of creating visually patterned prose. Thus, although art criticism may have been the first form of nonfiction to attempt a phenomenology of experience, the novels of Ann Radcliffe had managed to create one decades earlier.[2] The poetry of Wordsworth, which had a great influence upon Ruskin, also helped advance the development of experiential prose.[3] Ruskin, who developed several forms of visually oriented prose, relied upon word-painting from the beginning to the end of his career, and he almost always employed it within the sage's characteristic rhythm of satire and vision or positive example.

The simplest kind of Ruskinian and other word-painting takes the form of following one set or series of visual details by others in no particular order, whereas a second kind establishes a seeing or camera eye before which move various elements of a scene.[4]

[1]"Art Criticism as a Prose Genre," in *The Art of Victorian Prose*, ed. George Levine and Lionel Madden (New York, Oxford University Press, 1969), p. 39.

[2]See Rhoda L. Flaxman, "Victorian Word-Painting and Narrative: Toward the Blending of Genres" (Brown University Ph.D. dissertation, 1982), pp. 12–27.

[3]See James A. W. Heffernan, *The Re-Creation of Landscape: A Study of Wordsworth, Coleridge, Constable, and Turner* (Hanover, N.H., University Press of New England, 1985).

[4]For a Ruskinian example of the first or additive style of word-painting and the second, which employs a moving element within a scene, see the first volume of *Modern Painters*, 3.565, 395. I have discussed these forms of his word-painting in "There Began to Be a Great Talking about the Fine Arts," in *The Mind and Art of Victorian England*, ed. Josef L. Altholz (Minneapolis, University

Ruskin's third characteristic technique, which produces what we may anachronistically term a cinematic prose, proceeds by first establishing a center of consciousness that organizes the scene like a camera lens. Having established his narrative center or fictive eye, he then moves it either through or across his described scene—that is, he either turns this camera eye upon its axis, in effect panning across the scene, or else he changes the perceiving eye's distance to the scene, moving it closer (or into) the scene, or farther away to provide a distant view. Such literary strategies provide verbal art with a means of composing and ordering a linguistic description, thereby endowing it with some of the elements and capacities of the visual arts. This inevitably kinetic description possesses an energy that merely additive and accumulatory forms do not. Examples of this third, or proto-cinematic, form of word-painting in Ruskin's works include his elaborate description of La Riccia (3.278–80) in the first volume of *Modern Painters* (1843), his satiric look at Claude's *Il Mulino* and the Roman scenery it purports to depict in the 1844 preface to that same volume (3.41–43), and many passages in *The Stones of Venice* (1851–53), particularly his tour of St. Mark's (10.17–19), his narrative of the approach to Torcello (10.79–90), and his aerial view of the Mediterranean Sea (10.186–87).

All three forms of word-painting match Ruskin's own description of truly imaginative landscape representation. Several passages in *Modern Painters* explain that both the novice and the painter without imagination must content themselves with a merely topographical art of visual fact. According to the fourth volume of *Modern Painters*, "The aim of the great inventive landscape painter," in contrast, "must be to give the far higher and deeper truth of mental vision, rather than that of the physical facts, and to reach a representation which . . . shall yet be capable of producing on the far-away beholder's mind precisely the impression which the reality would have produced" (6.35). In this higher form of art, Ruskin says, "the artist not only *places*

---

of Minnesota Press, 1976), pp. 138–39. For an example of Lawrence's use of a moving element to compose a word-painting, see below, page 139.

the spectator, but . . . makes him a sharer in his own strong feelings and quick thoughts" (3.134). In other words, the great imaginative artist, whether he works in words or in paint, grants us the privilege of momentarily seeing with his eyes and imaginative vision: We experience his phenomenological relation to the world.

For Ruskin, as for other sages who employ such word-painting, these passages of highly wrought prose function within a larger structure of argument. In particular, they serve as a major part of that complex rhythm of satire and romantic vision that characterizes the proceedings of the sage. In the earlier volumes of *Modern Painters*, for example, where Ruskin employs it to defend Turner against the claims of older art, this structure first presents a satirical word-painting of a work by an old master and then follows it by one either of a relevant work by Turner or of a scene the older work was supposed to represent. The chapter "Of the Truth of Colour," in the first volume, begins by looking at Gaspar Poussin's *La Riccia* in the National Gallery, after which Ruskin presents his own impressions of the original scene. Writing with heavy sarcasm, he easily conveys the impression that Poussin's painting reveals little concern with presenting the facts of a particular place.

> It is a town on a hill, wooded with two-and-thirty bushes, of very uniform size, and possessing about the same number of leaves each. These bushes are all painted in with one dull opaque brown, becoming very slightly greenish towards the lights, and discover in one place a bit of rock, which of course would in nature have been cool and grey beside the lustrous hues of foliage, and which, therefore, being moreover completely in shade, is consistently and scientifically painted of a very clear, pretty, and positive brick red, the only thing like colour in the picture. The foreground is a piece of road which, in order to make allowance for its greater nearness, for its being completely in light, and, it may be presumed, for the quantity of vegetation usually present on carriage-roads, is given in a very cool green grey; and the truth of the picture is completed by a number of dots in the sky on the right, with a stalk to them of a sober and similar brown. (3.277–78)

Immediately after this harshly sarcastic rendering, Ruskin employs his familiar strategy of drawing upon his own experience of a scene that a work of art has presented. He begins by citing autobiography in order to certify the authenticity of the experience he is about to narrate: "Not long ago," he tells us, "I was slowly descending this very bit of carriage-road, the first turn after you leave Albano." Ruskin, who always emphasizes the change, variety, and energy of nature, then provides metereological fact that conveys the effect of a scene suffused with such energy and motion: "It had been wild weather when I left Rome, and all across the Campagna the clouds were sweeping in sulphurous blue, with a clap of thunder or two, and breaking gleams of sun along the Claudian aqueduct lighting up the infinity of its arches like the bridge of chaos." Having thus sketched in the background of his word picture, he presents himself moving upward through the scene until he catches sight of another vision of beauty in movement. "As I climbed the long slope of the Alban Mount, the storm swept finally to the north, and the noble outline of the domes of Albano, and the graceful darkness of its ilex grove, rose against pure streaks of alternate blue and amber; the upper sky gradually flushing through the last fragments of rain-cloud in deep palpitating azure, half aether and half dew." At this point, Ruskin, as he so often does, follows the path of light irradiating a landscape: "The noonday sun came slanting down the rocky slopes of La Riccia, and their masses of entangled and tall foliage, whose autumnal tints were mixed with the wet verdure of a thousand evergreens, were penetrated with it as with rain." Having thus led us to a Ruskinian epiphany, a Ruskinian vision of the earthly paradise, he sets before us a scene that combines all the beauty and sublimity of earth, sea, and heavens:

I cannot call it colour, it was conflagration. Purple, and crimson, and scarlet, like the curtains of God's tabernacle, the rejoicing trees sank into the valley in showers of light, every separate leaf quivering with buoyant and burning life; each, as it turned to reflect or to transmit the sunbeam, first a torch and then an emerald. Far up into the recesses of the valley, the green vistas arched like the hollows of mighty waves of some crystalline sea, with the arbutus flowers dashed along their flanks for foam, and silver flakes of orange spray tossed into the air around them, breaking over the grey walls of rock into a thousand separate stars, fading and kindling alternately as the weak wind lifted and let them fall. Every glade of grass burned like the golden floor of heaven, opening in sudden gleams as the foliage broke and closed above it, as sheet-lightning opens in a cloud at sunset. (3.278–79)

Here as elsewhere, Ruskin convinces us of his position by means of a superbly controlled alternation of vision and satire, preparing us for his polemic at each step of the way by allowing us to borrow his eyes and see. His skill at presenting us with his experience of landscape and landscape art continually makes us believe that his critical opponents and the painters he attacks both work from theory, from recipes, rather than from vision. In thus demonstrating his superiority to the critics of Turner, Ruskin proves himself a master of experience several times over. At the very least, he has described to us an Italian scene that we cannot otherwise experience without traveling to that location. Second, he has shared with us his own deeply felt experience of a particularly beautiful landscape. But as we read his narration of that experience—and Ruskin's presentations of such landscapes take the form, we remember, of narrations and not static descriptions—we realize that few, if any, of us could have perceived this scene so intensely. Ruskin, following his own prescriptions for imaginative art, has made us "a sharer in his own strong feelings and quick thoughts," and we also realize that the astonishing energy and movement of his mind, which appear in his lightning-fast associations, metaphors, and other analogies, match those of the scene he presents. In other words, unlike us, he is adequate to the experience. Finally, his presentation of landscape experience, which makes clear that he has true vision and the opposing critics are blinded by convention and insensitivity, also goes beyond beautiful description and presents a spiritual promise, an authentic visionary moment. In thus making us see and feel—in a word, experience—a divine presence in nature, Ruskin demonstrates that visual imperceptiveness, such as that which afflicts the critics of Turner, does society more harm than merely destroying taste. It prevents us from authentically experiencing the natural world, thereby robbing us of pleasure and solace, and furthermore, it contributes to spiritual blindness or insensitivity as well, since it keeps us from experiencing God in nature.

D. H. Lawrence learned from the author of *Modern Painters* and *The Stones of Venice* various modes of visually oriented prose, just as he also learned to transform Ruskinian word-painting into symbolic or mythological set pieces. But, as we shall observe, although many passages of Lawrence's writing, both in the travel books and in the fiction, clearly bear the impress of Ruskin the word-painter, many also extend these techniques into a new way of seeing, thinking, and feeling in prose.

In *Twilight in Italy* Lawrence uses the kind of word-painting that produces the effect of moving elements within a scene to describe his experience upon leaving the darkened, sensual interior of San Tommaso and coming out suddenly into bright day:

> Across, the heavy mountain crouched, along the side of the lake, the upper half brilliantly white, belonging to the sky, the lower half dark and grim. So, then, that is where heaven and earth are divided. From behind me, on the left, the headland swept down out of a great, pale-grey, arid height, through a rush of russet and crimson, to the olive smoke and the water of the level earth. And between, like a blade of the sky cleaving the earth asunder, went the pale-blue lake, cleaving mountain from mountain with the triumph of the sky.[5]

As this passage demonstrates, Lawrence, like Ruskin, creates his powerful descriptions by transforming description into narrative. In this instance he first implicitly places himself as viewer with the word *Across*, which informs the reader where the scene takes place in relation to the perceiving eye. Then Lawrence presents the outlines of mountain form, not as static boundaries between material masses but rather as paths of movement. Thus, the

---

[5]*Twilight in Italy* (London, William Heinemann, 1956), p. 22. Hereafter cited in text.

mountain "crouched" before him alongside the lake, while on his left hand the headland "swept down" from the arid heights. Since Lessing it has been a critical commonplace that the verbal arts are essentially temporal and the visual ones static. Ruskinian—and Laurentian—word-painting uses this inevitable sequentiality of verbal art both to order and to energize its attempts to create a visualizable pictorial image.

Another way that Lawrence metamorphoses description into narrative appears in the magnificent opening pages of "San Gaudenzio" in *Twilight in Italy*:

> The days go by, through the brief silence of winter, when the sunshine is so still and pure, like iced wine, and the dead leaves gleam brown, and water sounds hoarse in the ravines. It is so still and transcendent, the cypress trees poise like flames of forgotten darkness, that should have been blown out at the end of summer. For as we have candles to light the darkness of night, so the cypresses are candles to keep the darkness aflame in the full sunshine.
>
> Meanwhile, the Christmas roses become many. They rise from their budded, intact humbleness near the ground, they rise up, they throw up their crystal, they become handsome, they are heaps of confident, mysterious whiteness in the shadow of a rocky stream. It is almost uncanny to see them. They are the flowers of darkness, white and wonderful beyond belief.
>
> Then their radiance becomes soiled and brown, they thaw, break, and scatter and vanish away. Already the primroses are coming out, and the almond is in bud. The winter is passing away. On the mountains the fierce snow gleams apricot gold as evening approaches, golden, apricot, but so bright that it is almost frightening. What can be so fiercely gleaming when all is shadowy? It is something inhuman and unmitigated between heaven and earth. (81–82)

In this passage Lawrence neither includes a natural element, such as a stream, which moves through the scene to create movement, nor does he, as in the San Tommaso prospect vision, transform static visual elements into kinetic ones to produce the same effect. Rather he presents the transformation of scene in

140

the course of the seasons almost purely in terms of a narrative of change.

Compare his description of Cagliari in the closing pages of the section entitled "The Sea" in *Sea and Sardinia*. Like Ruskin's many descriptions of mountain scenery both in his autobiographical and in his art critical writings, this passage takes the form of a sudden sight, a moment of visual perception felt as a moment of spiritual or imaginative vision as well.

> And suddenly there is Cagliari: a naked town *rising* steep, steep, golden-looking, *piled* naked to the sky from the plain at the head of the formless hollow bay. It is strange and rather wonderful, not a bit like Italy. The city *piles up* lofty and almost miniature, and makes me think of Jerusalem: without trees, without cover, *rising* rather bare and proud, remote as if back in history, like a town in a monkish, illuminated missal ... rather jewel-like: like a sudden rose-cut amber jewel naked at the depth of the vast indenture. The air is cold, blowing bleak and bitter, the sky is all curd. And that is Cagliari. It has that curious look, as if it could be seen, but not entered. It is like some vision, some memory, something that has passed away. (52; emphasis added)

In one sense, Lawrence relates the experience of first seeing Cagliari much in the manner of a nineteenth-century traveler in search of the picturesque, for he proceeds by interspersing facts encountered with thoughts prompted by them.[6] This passage's presentation of a prospect vision and its comparison of that view to both a medieval missal and the New Jerusalem also resemble many parts of *Modern Painters* and *Praeterita*. This Ruskinian prospect vision, one immediately recognizes, derives its energy from its active verbs, but it is not composed in visual terms as is the description of the mountain view from San Tommaso, for

---

[6]Billy T. Tracy, "The Failure of the Flight: D. H. Lawrence's Travels," *Denver Quarterly* 12 (Spring 1977): 205–17; his "'Reading up the Ancient Etruscans': Lawrence's Debt to George Dennis," *Twentieth-Century Literature* 23 (December 1977): 437–50; and his *D. H. Lawrence and the Literature of Travel* (Ann Arbor, UMI Research Press, 1983), provide interesting background to Lawrence's use of the tradition of travel writing. Elizabeth K. Helsinger, *Ruskin and the Art of the Beholder* (Cambridge, Harvard University Press, 1982), provides a similar discussion of Ruskin in this context.

Lawrence presents the viewer looking at a scene rather than place him within it.

Lawrence's natural development of Ruskinian word-painting takes the form of using such techniques learned from his Victorian master to convey precisely those experiential and imaginative truths that most concerned him—and in so doing he advanced both nonfiction and the novel into new areas. Lawrence's own brilliant additions to the tradition of Ruskinian word-painting—the sensuous and semi-conscious feelings one experiences within a scene—appear with particular clarity in *Twilight in Italy* when he relates his experience of San Tommaso. This passage, which appears in "The Spinner and the Monks," owes a great deal to Ruskin's many presentations of prospect visions, Pisgah Sights, and distant views of mountains throughout his works (but particularly in *Modern Painters* and *Praeterita*), and that section which tells of Lawrence's entrance into the church itself seems based upon Ruskin's elaborate narrative presentation of St. Mark's in *The Stones of Venice*. After explaining that the "tiny chaotic back-ways" and "tortuous, tiny, deep passages of the village" (*Twilight in Italy*, 20) baffled him, Lawrence relates how, one day, he at last manages to ascend to the church that surmounts the village. Finding a broken stairway, he runs up it, "and came out suddenly, as by a miracle, clean on the platform of my San Tommaso, in the tremendous sunshine," and he discovers himself in "another world, the world of the eagle, the world of fierce abstraction. . . . I was in the skies now" (21). After describing his setting, first in terms of the details surrounding him and then by filling in the distant sights far below on the lake, Lawrence next ruminates upon the church he has come to investigate, after which he enters its sheltering darkness.

> It always remains to me that San Tommaso and its terrace hang suspended above the village, like the lowest step of heaven, of Jacob's ladder. Behind, the land rises in a high sweep. But the terrace of San Tommaso is let down from heaven, and does not touch the earth.
>
> I went into the Church. It was very dark, and impregnated with centuries of incense. It affected me like the lair of some enormous

creature. My senses were roused, they sprang awake in the hot, spiced darkness. My skin was expectant, as if it expected some contact, some embrace, as if it were aware of the contiguity of the physical world, the physical contact with the darkness and the heavy, suggestive substance of the enclosure. It was a thick, fierce darkness of the senses. But my soul shrank.

I went out again. The pavemented threshold was clear as a jewel, the marvellous clarity of sunshine that becomes blue in the height seemed to distill me into it. (21–22)

This passage well exemplifies Lawrence's version of what Richard L. Stein has taught us to recognize as a Ruskinian "fable of perception."[7] Brilliantly as this scene departs from Ruskin's own methods by emphasizing the physical and subconscious reactions of the viewer, it nonetheless represents Lawrence adding to instead of denying his Ruskinian heritage.

In fact, Lawrence here stands in relation to Ruskin as Ruskin himself stands in relation to Sir Joshua Reynolds; each incorporates and builds upon the ideas of his predecessor. When Reynolds attempted to win prestige for the art of painting, he found himself forced to use the only available terminology, and he therefore employed the traditional opposition between mechanical (or physical) and intellectual arts. Thus he claimed that painting, like literature, was an intellectual art. In contrast, Ruskin inherited the resources of the romantic tradition, and when he came to formulate his romantic theory of the sister arts—he takes literature and painting as equivalent forms of the poetic and urges us to receive his remarks on one subject as applying to the other—he added a third term, the imaginative, to the two that Reynolds had used. Therefore, he can urge that in contrast to works produced by physical and intellectual means, poetry is produced by the higher faculty of imagination. Lawrence, who comfortably takes his place in this progression, demonstrates by his descriptive passages and narrative that he adds the unconscious and sexual drives to those faculties Ruskin had described. For Lawrence, therefore, imaginative description had to include

---

[7]*The Ritual of Interpretation* (Cambridge, Harvard University Press, 1975), p. 53.

those sensations that hover around and beneath consciousness. By including and even emphasizing elements that Ruskin had himself not included, Lawrence extends this kind of imaginative description in his own way. Such a history of the evolution of word-painting and its theoretical roots sounds suspiciously like one of those purely progressive histories of style or other phenomena that always present what comes later as superior to what preceded it. Of course, from the point of view of one who considers Lawrence's kinds of additions to descriptive prose to be the finest things such prose can produce, this conclusion would be valid. Others have to point out, however, that Laurentian description sacrifices one kind of strength for another. Therefore, the only kind of progressive history his contributions to word-painting support is one that holds that styles or modes must continually develop different capacities.

Like Lawrence, Mailer makes use of elaborate set pieces of this literature of experience in *Of a Fire on the Moon* both to advance his argument and to create credibility for his interpretations of what he takes to be a major event of our times. In fact, his main concerns demand that he demonstrate his ability both to think and to feel, in order to demonstrate to himself and to his audience that he has a message, that his interpretations have authenticity in this age of the pervasively inauthentic. *Of a Fire on the Moon* narrates his attempt to use the first voyage to the moon to answer his own questions about the true relations of technology to the possibilities of heroism, the existence of powerful experience in a mechanical, dehumanizing age, and the simple adequacy of language and experience to each other in the seventh decade of the twentieth century. Therefore to authenticate his own project he must first encounter—and prove to us that he has encountered—powerful, soul-stirring events, and to do so he writes in the guise of the master of experience.

His presentation of the moment of liftoff, which takes the form of a narrative meditation upon it, well exemplifies Mailer's masterful use of his own feelings and imagination as a guide to the reader. He begins with the moment of expectant seeing and immediately places that moment within the prophetic context: "He had his binoculars to his eyes. A tiny part of him was like a penitent who had prayed in the wilderness for sixteen days and was now expecting a sign. Would the sign reveal much or little?" (98). Would the sign in fact come at all, and if it came would it reveal the entire enterprise of the expedition to the moon as a crucial event, a worthy happening, or would it turn out to be just another banal nonevent of the narcotized twentieth century? At this point he includes a transcript of the words spoken by Apollo-Saturn Launch Control during the last few minutes before the launch, including the final seconds of countdown, and then begins the narration of his own experience of viewing it.

But nobody watching the launch from the Press Site ever listened to the last few words. For at 8.9 seconds before lift-off, the motors of the Apollo-Saturn leaped into ignition, and two horns of orange fire burst like genies from the base of the rocket. Aquarius never had to worry again about whether the experience would be appropriate to his measure. Because of the distance, no one at the Press Site was to hear the sound of the motors until fifteen seconds after they had started. Although the rocket was restrained on its pad for nine seconds in order for the motors to multiply up to full thrust, the result was still that the rocket began to rise a full six seconds before its motors could be heard. Therefore the lift-off itself seemed to partake more of a miracle than a mechanical phenomenon, as if all of huge Saturn itself had begun silently to levitate, and was then pursued by flames. (99)

Mailer in the guise of Aquarius here presents what he saw during the first seconds of liftoff, and he makes clear that it has answered his first, basic question—a question that he has made ours as well—and that this phenomenon, this Sign of the Times, is an event of true power. He then employs intellectual, rational explanation to show why the viewers at first experience liftoff only in terms of the sense of sight, after which he relates his first impressions, that in its silent levitation the slowly rising rocket "seemed to partake more of a miracle than a mechanical phenomenon" and that it appeared "pursued by flames," instead of jetting them forth. Immediately after having thus introduced these fanciful descriptions and impressions, he then turns his back upon them: "No, it was more dramatic than that. For the

145

flames were enormous. No one could be prepared for that. Flames flew in cataract against the cusp of the flame shield, and then sluiced along the paved ground down two opposite channels in the concrete, two underground rivers of flame which poured into the air on either side a hundred feet away, then flew a hundred feet further" (99–100). Mailer here employs the ancient literary device of denied comparison. After presenting his first descriptions and analogies, he denies their validity and replaces them by others. Centuries earlier Shakespeare began one of his sonnets, "Shall I compare thee to a summer's day?" after which he answered his own query with a similiar denial that obviously implied that conventional language and expression were inadequate to his subject. By showing the reader of his sonnet all the ways that the young man to whom he addressed his poem surpasses a summer's day, he could enjoy all the power provided by conventional descriptions and stock analogies, including instant comprehension, without having to accept responsibility for them. At the same time the poet effortlessly demonstrated that conventionalities failed to capture the beauty of his subject, which lay far beyond them and demanded a new, more accurate language. Mailer achieves precisely the same effect when he suddenly changes direction in the midst of his experiential fable.

His use of denied comparison also achieves another effect vital to creating credibility, for such a pattern of suggestion and denial produces the effect (rather, the illusion) of the authorial mind groping toward the comprehension and expression of a difficult truth. Mailer wants readers to receive the impression of a Mailer so committed to communicating exactly what he has experienced, so committed to truth, that he willingly permits them inside his consciousness and allows them to observe him making mistakes and energetically correcting them. He wants them to receive the impression, in other words, of a powerful, *honest*, mind in action. Like Ruskin and Lawrence, Mailer employs this pattern in dramatizing the experience of perception as a crucial stage in his argument. Since the experience of interpretation plays as crucial a role in our lives as the sheer isolated physical experience itself, Mailer appropriately continues his dramatization by relating how he first gropingly tried to embrace

the meaning of the event he was observing. He thereupon continues one of the dominant patterns of his narrative, which is
first to communicate an experience and then to offer an interpretation of it, by making elaborate comparisons between the huge
white rocket and Moby Dick, another American incarnation of
awesome power pervaded by moral and spiritual ambiguity.

At this point in the narration Mailer replaces the experience
of sight by that of sound, replaces the data provided by the more
intellectualizable, distancing sense of sight by the more basic,
more physically stirring senses of sound and motion.

Then it came, like a crackling of wood twigs over the ridge, came
with the sharp and furious bark of a million drops of oil crackling
suddenly into combustion, a cacophony of barks louder and louder
as Apollo-Saturn fifteen seconds ahead of its own sound cleared
the lift tower to a cheer which could have been a cry of anguish
from that near-audience watching; then came the earsplitting bark
of a thousand machine guns firing at once, and Aquarius shook
through his feet at the fury of this combat assault, and heard the
thunderous murmur of Niagaras of flame roaring conceivably louder
than the loudest thunders he had ever heard and the earth began
to shake and would not stop, it quivered through his feet standing
on the wood of the bleachers, an apocalyptic fury of sound equal
to some conception of the sound of your death in the roar of a
drowning hour, a nightmare of sound, and he heard himself
saying, "Oh, my God! oh, my God! oh, my God! oh, my God!
oh, my God! oh, my God!" but not his voice . . . and the sound
of the rocket beat with the true blood of fear in his ears. (100)

This dramatization of Mailer's experience of the liftoff, which so
effectively combines a narrative of sense perception with his first
tentative gropings at understanding that experience, perfectly
suits his strategy in *Of a Fire on the Moon*. Mailer, we recall,
goes through most of the crucial events of the moon voyage and
landing twice, first imaginatively outside and then inside the
events; that is, he first presents the awesome power and size of
the machines, after which he interprets the importance and
meaning of the events in which these machines played so promi-
nent a role.

147

But even before he arrives at that final interpretation, he returns to the moment of liftoff and explains the extraordinary complexity of that event itself. In essence, his narrative presentation of what occurs during the first seconds of launch provides the reader with an intellectual experience, as opposed to the earlier purely physical one, of the liftoff:

It was the life experience of such rocket engineers as Von Braun, rather than the laws of physics, which decreed that Apollo-Saturn be chained to its base until the thrust upward was a million two hundred thousand pounds greater than its weight. For that reason, it was manacled by four giant metal hold-down arms. You can be certain there had been cracks in the early forgings of test metals of the hold-down arms for they were not easy to design, being massive in size yet required to let go their million-pound grip on the split part of an instant. The unlatching interval for the four arms had to be all but simultaneous—the separation was geared not to exceed one-twentieth of a second for its duration: in fact if any of the four arms had failed to complete their operation in more than a fifth of a second, the liberation would have been effected by properly placed explosives.... even with all four hold-down arms sprung at once, the rocket ship was still restrained for the first few inches of travel. Something exactly so simple as eight tapered pins had each to be drawn through its own die—as the vehicle rose through the first six inches of flight, each die was obliged to straighten the taper in its own iron pin—the eight dies to travel up with the ship, the eight shucked pins to be left in their fastenings on the hold-down brackets. If not for such a simple mechanism, Apollo-Saturn might have leaped off its pad fast enough to set up a resonance, then a vibration strong enough to shake the ship and some thousands of its instruments too critically. For consider: if when empty, the space vessel weighed less than half a million pounds, it was now carrying a weight of fuel twelve times greater than itself. But there were no bones or muscles in this fuel, nothing in the fuel to hold the ship together, just liquids to slosh and shake and seek to distort the rigidity of the structure.... One would look to reduce every quiver in so delicate a structure—the restraining pins performed just such a function for the first half-foot of ascent.

In the course of this act, at an instant when the spaceship was

148

not yet three-quarters of an inch off the ground, specific switches
on the hold-down arms tripped loose a pneumatic system which
gave power to surges of compressed gas which ran in pipes up the
great height of the launching tower: the gas tripped the couplings
of the five service bridges still connected to the rocket. Their umbilicals now detatched, these arms pulled away as the ship began
to rise. Six inches up, and loose from the pins, the stages of Apollo-Saturn climbed up the stories of the Mobile Launcher, climbed
up on its self-created base of flame, up past the flying withdrawal
of its bridges and umbilicals. To clear the tower, to be free of any
sudden gust of wind which might lash it sideways, a yaw
maneuver, programmed into the rocket, was initiated one second
after lift-off, and turned the nose a few degrees from the vertical
farther way from the tower. For the onlookers three and one-half
miles away, the rocket appeared to waver, then stagger. In fact, it
did. There was wind blowing, and the rocket had been designed
not to fight wind (it was not stressed for that) but to give way to
wind, to relinquish the trajectory it was on, and compute a new
trajectory from the slightly different position where the gust had
left it. So separate commands kept issuing from the Instrument
Unit at the top of Saturn, sometimes every half-second, and the
motors kept responding with little spurts and sags of speed. . . .
[The rocket cleared the tower] after eight seconds. At close to
twelve seconds, the four outboard engines were swiveled through a
few degrees, a pitch maneuver was initiated, and a roll. The roll
would end in twenty seconds, the shift in pitch would continue for
two minutes and twenty-five seconds by which time the rocket
would be climbing no longer straight up. (211–13)

Mailer's superb technical writing here functions to enhance his
credibility in several ways. First, it obviously demonstrates that
he understands the often astonishing complexities of the technology involved in the moon program—and hence, whatever conclusions he draws upon its final meaning and value, the reader
will not be likely to attribute his conclusions to that hostility
that arises in ignorance and inability to comprehend. Second,
the sheer virtuosity of the writing, particularly its combination of
clear narrative with an ongoing explanatory commentary, produces another form of his dramatization of experience. Here
Mailer does not use his descriptive powers to communicate an ex-

perience of awesome sublimity and power. Rather he presents the experience of understanding, placing the reader within an ideal intellectual vantage point where the time that obtains is that of science and technology and not that of the pulses.

Tom Wolfe uses his skill at this kind of writing to convey the experience of another version of the technological sublime in "The Truest Sport: Jousting with Sam and Charlie," an essay he drew upon for *The Right Stuff*. Tom Wolfe's presentation of this kind of experiential prose differs markedly from that of Mailer, who follows Ruskin and Lawrence in relying upon an idealized author as the focus of narrated experience. Mailer, however, forces himself upon the reader far more than do his predecessors. Of course, Ruskin's quotations of his own diaries and citations of his own experience make clear that he expects the reader to take this idealized presence as Ruskin himself, but in most passages he places his chief emphasis upon the scene and not upon himself. Mailer, in contrast, thrusts himself (in the guise of Aquarius) to the fore and insists that the reader perceive every scene with him in the foreground.

Wolfe, who creates a very different effect by avoiding such an authorial persona or voice, instead divides his fables of experience among a range of voices, some of which can be taken for the author himself while others represent fictionalized surrogates for our experience. The specific occasion for creating a fable of experience is Wolfe's desire to convey the difficulty, terror, and heroism of flying a jet fighter from the pitching, heaving deck of an aircraft carrier. He begins by presenting the experience from the viewpoint of an old hand, and then, as he so frequently does, he shifts this viewpoint and presents the scene from that of the newcomer, moving closer in several stages. In the first of these he presents the neophyte's reactions with third-person narration, after which he uses the first person as if he were the neophyte himself speaking. According to Wolfe's narrator, when the neophyte first steps onto the catwalk that leads to the flight deck, "right away the burglar alarm sounds in his central nervous system. Listen, Skipper!—the integrity of the circuit has been violated somewhere."[8] Looking over

[8]"The Truest Sport: Jousting with Sam and Charlie," in *Mauve Gloves &*

the railing of the catwalk he sees that it is a six-story drop to water that looks like steel, and meanwhile the horizon is heaving
up and down. Clambering finally to the flight deck itself, the
neophyte, whom Wolfe clearly intends to function as our surro-
gate for this terrifying experience, discovers that it has little resemblance to the enormous piece of gray geometry it had in the
training film: "Geometry—by God, man, this is a . . . skillet! It
heaves, it moves up and down underneath his feet, it pitches up,
it pitches down." As the wind sweeps across this deck sixty feet
above the sea, we realize that it has no railings to keep us from
being swept overboard and that there is also "no way whatsoever
to cry out to another living soul for a helping hand, because on
top of everything else the newcomer realizes that his sense of
hearing has been *amputated entirely*." The deck itself, on which
people run about in odd costumes, strikes us with such a sensory
overload that we can barely take it in, much less imagine per-
forming some appointed function on it.

This is a *skillet!*—a frying pan!—a short-order grill!—not gray but
black, smeared with skid marks from one end to the other and glis-
tening with pools of hydraulic fluid and the occasional jet-fuel
slick, all of it still hot, sticky, greasy, runny, virulent from God
knows what traumas—still ablaze!—consumed in detonations, ex-
plosions, flames, combustion, roars, shrieks, whines, blasts, cy-
clones, dust storms, horrible shudders, fracturing impacts, all of it
taking place out on the very edge of control, if in fact it can be
contained at all, which seems extremely doubtful, because the
whole scorched skillet is still *heaving* up and down the horizon and
little men . . . are skittering about on the surface as if for their
very lives (you've said it now!), clustering about twin-engine F-4
fighter planes likes bees about the queen, . . . and then running for
cover as the two jet engines go into their shriek and a huge
deflection plate rises up behind the plane because it is about to go
into its explosion and quite enough gets blown . . . off this heaving grill as it is, and then they explode into full afterburn, 37,000
pounds of force, and a very storm of flames, heat, crazed winds,

Madmen, Clutter & Vine (New York, Farrar, Straus and Giroux, 1976), pp.
29–30. The passages quoted below appear on pp. 30–32.

151

and a billion blown steely particles—a very storm engulfs the deck, followed by an unbelievable shudder—*kaboom!*—that pounds through the skillet and destroys whatever may be left of the neophyte's vestibular system, and the howling monster is flung up the deck . . . and the F-4 is launched.

Immediately after submitting us to this experience, Wolfe tries to surpass it in revealing that the neophyte's fear (our fear!) is even more intense when the jets return for landing, for although we might believe that a plane glides onto a runway, when standing upon a heaving deck one knows that is not the case. As the plane's speed does not diminish, "one experiences a neural alarm he has never in his wildest fears imagined before: this is not an *air*plane coming toward me, it's a brick, and it is not *gliding*, it's *falling*, a fifty-thousand-pound brick, headed not for a stripe on the deck, but for *me*—and with a horrible *smash!* it hits the skillet," and hurtles toward the end of the deck, engines screaming as the pilot accelerates them in case he needs to attempt an emergency takeoff. One next experiences a tremendous shudder as twenty-five tons smash upon the heaving metal deck as the plane jerks to an abrupt halt.

Wolfe, like other masters of experience, works to place us inside a situation that we would otherwise find unlikely or even impossible to encounter. Unlike travel writing, which had an influence upon early practitioners of this technique, these experiential passages occur within a larger argument. Wolfe examines the relations of heroism, status, and technology in the lives of fighter pilots hurled from the decks of aircraft carriers, just as Mailer similarly explores the nature of heroism in the midst of technology. Heroism in these modern works has much the same meaning that it does in ancient authors. It provides us with a means of exploring the limits of humanity and formulating an ideal that serves as a norm by which to judge our acts and our hopes. The master of experience who lends us his memory and imagination so that we can better understand these high matters also appears as a hero, an ideal, at the same time that he mediates between the higher human natures and ourselves. Like Ruskin and Lawrence, recent practitioners of this technique or approach offer extreme experiences that are otherwise un-obtainable—those of terror and beauty, energy and sublimity. In so doing, the sage who presents himself as a master of experience inevitably gains stature in the eyes of his audience, for not only can he make its members feel more alive but he can also enable them to understand new matters as well. As we shall observe in the next chapter, such presentations of himself as master of experience represent only one of the sage's many ways of achieving *ethos*, the appeal to credibility.

5

Ethos, or the Appeal to Credibility

The Ethos of the Sage and the Ethos of Fiction

Rhetoricians have traditionally held that one can argue by means of *logos*, the appeal to logic or reason; *pathos*, the appeal to emotion; or *ethos*, the appeal to credibility. As Aristotle explains in the first chapter of the *Rhetoric* (1356a), "Persuasion is achieved by the speaker's personal character when the speech is so spoken as to make us think him credible. We believe good men more fully and more readily than others: this is true generally whatever the question is, and absolutely true where exact certainty is impossible and opinions are divided." Aristotle, who emphasizes that ethos "should be achieved by what the speaker says" and not by his reputation prior to speaking, concludes that character or ethos "may almost be called the most effective means of persuasion."[1]

[1]*Rhetorica*, trans. W. Rhys Roberts, in *The Basic Works of Aristotle*, ed. Richard McKeon (New York, Random House, 1941), p. 1329. The Lane Cooper translation renders this passage as follows: "The character [ethos] of the speaker is a cause of persuasion when the speech is so uttered as to make him worthy of belief; for as a rule we trust men of probity more, and more quickly, about things in general, while on points outside the realm of exact knowledge, where opinion is divided, we trust them absolutely. This trust, however, should be created by

154

Of course, all argumentation tries to convince the listener or reader that the speaker deserves credence, and every convincing instance of logic, authority, or testimony demonstrates that he has earned it. But the writings of the sage are unique in that their central or basic rhetorical effect is the implicit statement to the audience: "I deserve your attention and credence, for I can be trusted, and no matter how bizarre my ideas or my interpretations may at first seem, they deserve your respect, your attention, and ultimately your allegiance because they are correct and they are necessary to your well-being." This appeal to credibility, of course, plays some role in any kind of literary mode or form of argumentation that attempts to convince someone of something, but only in the writings of the sage does ethos become the principal effect, and not merely a contributory one. Ethos and the various techniques that produce it are hardly unique to this genre.[2] What is unique, however, is the central importance of the appeal to credibility, which subsumes the sage's other rhetorical devices. In essence, one might define the genre of the sage as that in which evidentiary and other appeals function only to produce such confidence in a speaker or writer that he can be believed when

the speech itself, and not left to depend upon an antecedent impression that the speaker is that or that kind of man. It is not true, as some writers on the art maintain, that the probity of the speaker contributes nothing to his persuasiveness; on the contrary, we might almost affirm that his character [ethos] is the most potent of all the means to persuasion" (*The Rhetoric* [New York, Appleton, 1960], pp. 8–9; quoted by Seymour Chatman, *Story and Discourse: Narrative Structure in Fiction and Film* [Ithaca, Cornell University Press, 1978], pp. 226–27).

[2]Baruch Hochman, *Character in Literature* (Ithaca, Cornell University Press, 1985), explains some of the ultimate sources of ethos when he argues that characters in literature, narrators, and "people in life . . . have in common . . . the model, which we carry in our heads, of what a person is. Both characters and people are apprehended in someone's consciousness, and they are apprehended in approximately the same terms" (7). According to Hochman, "Since speech implies a speaker, literary speech suggests to us the character of the speaker, whether that speaker is the narrator of *Tom Jones* or the voice that 'utters' a lyric poem" (8). If "speech" (and written discourse) thus inevitably generate a sense of character, specific styles of speech generate an equally specific, individualized sense of that character. Writing of Rabelais, Flaubert, and Shakespeare, Hochman comments: "What happens in each of these vastly different instances is that a recognizable rhetorical mode is elaborated to the point where a character emerges, often with the aid of actions and gestures wholly congruous with his or her speech" (73).

155

conventional wisdom, supposedly expert testimony, or one's incli-
nation argues against his position.

After briefly comparing the sage's ethos to that of the narrative
voice in Victorian fiction, I propose to suggest the ways that the
sage's techniques at which we have already looked work to create
credibility. Then, after sketching a taxonomy of techniques that
produce ethos, I shall concentrate on those central ones involving
autobiography and self-revelation that attempt to authenticate the
sage's message by authenticating the sage himself. Finally, citing
examples from the writings of Didion and Mailer, I shall show how
techniques that strive to create this effect of credibility function to
create an equivalent to plot in fiction.

Although many of the greatest Victorian novels employ techniques that create ethos, they do so for quite different purposes
than do works of the sage.[3] Whereas Carlyle, Ruskin, and Arnold
rely upon the appeal to credibility as a means of urging the reader
to accept their judgments, Dickens, Thackeray, and Trollope use it
to make the reader accept the judgments of their novels' narrators,
and these judgments in turn enable the reader to evaluate characters and events. Ethos in the novel thus works at one remove from
the actual author. Of course, not all novels employ (or create)
ethos—only those that have an implied author who makes use of
extensive commentary.

Such commentary plays an important role in fiction and shapes
much of the reader's experience. As Geoffrey Tillotson pointed out
more than three decades ago in his study of Thackeray, reading
that novelist involves more than an encounter with narrative and
description: "If, while reading Thackeray, we look into the composition of our experience, we find that a portion of it, even while
the narration is at its purest, is experience of commentary."[4] The

---

[3]As this study was going to press, I discovered Chatman's assertion that "Ethos
also functions in fictional narrative, except that its standard is not truth but veri-
similitude, the semblance of veracity. . . . Since a narrative never communicates
the direct speech of the implied author, ethos can only apply to a narrator." According to Chatman, "the narrator's rhetorical effort is to prove that his version
of the story is true" (*Story and Discourse*, 227). In contrast, as I argue below,
ethos in the novel has a broader effect.

[4]Geoffrey Tillotson, *Thackeray the Novelist* (1954) (London, Methuen, 1963),
p. 91. Tillotson further points out that Thackeray "is the critic, not merely of cer-

evidence of Victorian and modern readers proves that this kind of commentary, which until quite recently was thought to exemplify "non-novelistic" and inartistic elements, provides an important part of the pleasure of reading a novel and cannot therefore be considered necessarily extraneous to it. Wayne Booth correctly argues in *The Rhetoric of Fiction* that if our criterion for allowing authorial commentary is "appropriateness to the whole work, we are forced to ask ourselves what the 'whole work' is when dozens of pages have already been devoted to commentary. We do not experience these 'intrusions' as independent outbursts; they are continuing steps in our acquaintance with the narrator."[5]

Acquaintance with the narrators of Victorian novels provides a major source of these books' pleasure. Unfortunately for critical understanding of this kind of fictional effect, the emphasis upon indirection and avoiding authorial commentary made by Percy Lubbock's influential *The Craft of Fiction* (1921), which dominated criticism of the novel in England and America for four decades, simply led critics to deny the critical validity of narrative comment and refuse to take seriously the remarks of those who claimed to receive pleasure from it. Not surprisingly, this reductive neo-Jamesian approach to the novel assumes that readers who enjoy authorial commentary are naive and critically uninformed. In contrast, Booth, who argues that authorial commentary is inevitable, accepts the testimony of readers. In particular, he cites as the kind of evidence a critical theory of fiction must take into account remarks by readers that they enjoy the narrators of Eliot, Dickens, Forster.[6] Booth specifically raises this subject because it contributes to our understanding of the role played in fiction by the implied author's commentary; the fictive personality of this implied author is created, we recall, by commentary. Booth's clear-

---

tain things, but of everything he invents. . . . Sometimes a critical idea runs hand in hand with the narrative for a long stretch" (91).

[5] *The Rhetoric of Fiction* (Chicago, University of Chicago Press, 1961), p. 208. Hereafter cited in text.

[6] Booth quotes, for instance, Clayton Hamilton, *Materials and Methods of Fiction* (London, Grant Richards, 1909), p. 132, who points out that "many readers return again and again to 'The Newcomes' not so much for the pleasure of seeing London high society as for the pleasure of seeing Thackeray see it" (213n). This note contains similar comments on Dickens and Forster by other critics.

headed approach also permits us to observe how Victorian fiction employs ethos.

Ethos-creating statements can take the form of either interspersed commentary or miniature essays. The twentieth chapter of George Eliot's *Middlemarch* provides an example of individual sentences of commentary that alternate with those containing narrative or description. When Eliot relates Dorothea Brooke's disorientation after she has encountered Rome, the implied author emphasizes the effect of "the gigantic broken revelations of that Imperial and Papal city thrust abruptly upon the notions of a girl who had been brought up on English and Swiss Puritanism."[7] Because this encounter is so important to understanding Dorothea, the novel provides a detailed analysis of her character in order to present us with the necessary context. At this point, the narrator of *Middlemarch* first makes a generalization about other young women and then describes the culture shock Dorothea experienced:

> The weight of unintelligible Rome might lie easily on bright nymphs to whom it formed a background for the brilliant picnic of Anglo-foreign society; but Dorothea had no such defence against deep impressions. Ruins and basilicas, palaces and colossi, set in the midst of a sordid present, where all that was living and warm-blooded seemed sunk in the deep degeneracy of a superstition divorced from reverence; the dimmer but yet eager Titanic life grazing and struggling on walls and ceilings; ... all this vast wreck of ambitious ideals, sensuous and spiritual, mixed confusedly with the signs of breathing forgetfulness and degradation, at first jarred her as with an electric shock, and then urged themselves on her with that ache belonging to a glut of confused ideas which check the flow of emotion. Forms both pale and glowing took possession of her young sense, and fixed themselves in her memory even when she was not thinking of them, preparing strange associations which remained through her after-years.

Immediately following these sentences relating Dorothea's disorien-

---

[7]For the background of Dorothea's encounter with Rome, see Hugh Witemeyer, *George Eliot and the Visual Arts* (New Haven, Yale University Press, 1979), pp. 79–87, and George P. Landow, "Victorianized Romans: Images of Rome in Victorian Painting," *Browning Institute Studies* 12 (1984): 29–51.

tation comes the kind of generalization that has long been consid-ered typical of George Eliot (and the implied authors of her nov-els): "Our moods are apt to bring with them images which succeed each other like the magic-lantern pictures in a doze." The conclud-ing portion of this sentence then applies this generalization to Dor-othea in the form of a narrative of her future, for we are told that "in certain states of dull forlornness Dorothea all her life continued to see the vastness of St Peter's ... spreading itself everywhere like a disease of the retina." Eliot's implied author moves back and forth among statements of narrative, description, and generalized truths that support the other two, providing them with a context and richer meaning, but that do not relate specifically to them.

In contrast to the way Eliot here intertwines sentences and even phrases of generalizing commentary with narrative and description, Trollope's *The Way We Live Now* contains wisdom statements that take the form of miniature essays.[8] Trollope's narrator here is com-menting upon those guests who eagerly attended Melmotte's ban-quet for the Emperor of China despite believing their host immoral and even criminal:

> There can be no doubt that the greater part of the people assem-bled did believe that their host had committed some great fraud which might probably bring him under the arm of the law. When such rumors are spread abroad, they are always believed. There is an excitement and a pleasure in believing them. Reasonable hesitation at such a moment is dull and phlegmatic. If the accused be one near enough to ourselves to make the accusation a matter of personal pain, of course we disbelieve. But, if the distance be beyond this, we are almost ready to think that anything may be true of anybody. In this case nobody really loved Melmotte and everybody did believe. It was so probable that such a man should have done something horri-ble! It was only hoped that the fraud might be great and horrible enough. (Chap. 62)

[8]Mary L. Daniels, *Trollope-to-Reader: A Topical Guide to Digressions in the Novels of Anthony Trollope* (Westport, Conn., Greenwood Press, 1983), which consists of passages from the novels arranged according to various more or less appropriate headings, provides a convenient means for examining the range of his commen-tary. Although Daniels does not distinguish between pure commentary and that intermingled with narrative, she offers an interesting arrangement by topic.

159

The first sentence in this paragraph, like the last three, comments directly upon the thoughts of characters whose actions are being narrated by the implied author. The five that follow, in contrast, form a kind of extractable essay that presents the narrator's understanding of how people act in general and not just in this specific case. One can make three observations about this Trollopean moral essay-in-miniature: First, it presents general truths that are not specific to the facts or situation being narrated. Second, it focuses our judgments of the events and actions presented by the implied author. As Wayne Booth points out, "any story will be unintelligible unless it includes, however subtly, the amount of telling necessary not only to make us aware of the value system which gives it its meaning but, more important, to make us willing to accept that value system, at least temporarily. . . . The work itself . . . must fill with its rhetoric the gap made by the suspension of my own beliefs" (112). The implied author's comments, in other words, provide necessary pointers to the reader, which, even if they do not change his mind completely about any particular moral or other judgment, nonetheless orient him and in this way inform him how to interpret a particular set of actions and ideas. Third, Trollope's brief essay on the way people delight in rumor also serves to build the reader's confidence in the implied author, who appears in such statements as a wisdom speaker.

Although such remarks will have their most positive effects when the reader accepts them as valid generalizations about human conduct, they work to an important degree even when he takes them only as witty, if cynical, observations and apothegms, and they do so because they inform the reader how the implied author wishes to be understood. In other words, such statements, which generations of readers have testified provide a great deal of the pleasure in the novels of Trollope, Eliot, Thackeray, and other Victorians, indicate both how readers should judge character and event and also how they should regard the presenter of them. Even if readers refuse to grant the narrator full credibility, even if they resist and reserve judgment, they at least do not feel at sea in the world of the novel.

Furthermore, even when the implied author presents attitudes and opinions with which the audience chooses not to agree, he

160

does not produce the sage's characteristically abrasive effect, for such generalizations rarely involve either the Victorian sage's aggressiveness and assumed superiority or the modern sage's equally aggressive thrusting of private weakness and intimate fact upon the reader.

Although the primary novelistic means of creating ethos involves the use of wisdom statements, a use which distinguishes novelistic ethos from that of the sage, occasionally Victorian fiction does employ means of producing it that resemble those of the sages. For example, as Booth points out, much novelistic commentary contributes to "our sense of traveling with a trustworthy companion, an author who is sincerely battling to do justice to his materials. George Eliot, for example, involves us constantly in her battle to deal with the truth" (214); and, writing of Melville's *Billy Budd*, Booth adds that "even the most clumsily worded intrusion can redeem itself by conveying this sense of how deeply the narrator cares about what he is doing" (215). In fact, as Booth suggests in passing, a novelist's attempts to ingratiate himself with the reader provide another kind of plot, one quite different from that of fiction but often necessary to it. Much of Fielding's commentary in *Tom Jones*, for example, "relates to nothing but the reader and himself," but such intrusion justifies itself on the grounds, argues Booth, that it shapes our "attitude toward the book as a whole" by providing "a running account of growing intimacy between the narrator and the reader, an account with a kind of plot of its own and a separate denouement" (216).

Wayne Booth's clarifying the role of commentary in Victorian and early fiction demonstrates that John Holloway was on firm ground when he claimed in *The Victorian Sage* that authors of fiction and nonfiction shared rhetorical techniques, for, like the sages, the narrators of many Victorian novels strive to create this effect of credibility. In fact, certain works of Victorian fiction—George Eliot's *Felix Holt* comes to mind—succeed to the extent that they do largely because of an interesting, trustworthy narrator and not because they have particularly effective characterization or plot.[9] *Holt* stands out as a particularly ineffective and in-

[9]For discussions of this novel see George Levine, "Introduction," to George

effectual protagonist, and yet Eliot's novel engages the reader, for like the writings of Carlyle and Arnold, its discursive sections successfully produce ethos. Nonetheless, I must emphasize once again that despite such important similarities between ethos in fiction and nonfiction, the appeals to credibility made by the narrator of *Felix Holt* differ in two ways from those in *Chartism, Unto This Last,* or *Culture and Anarchy.* First, although both literary forms create personae that represent idealized versions of the author, that in the writings of the sage remains much closer to the author himself and is clearly meant to be understood as being the author. Second, the kind of ethos sought by the major Victorian novelists is that of the traditional wisdom speaker whereas that sought by the sages is that of a contentious, alienated prophet. Eliot's narrator in *Felix Holt,* in other words, has far more in common with Emerson than with Carlyle and Thoreau.[10]

Techniques That Create Ethos

Many of the techniques at which we have already looked contribute to the sage's creation of ethos. First of all, brilliant interpretations, particularly of apparently inappropriate materials, work to transfer the audience's allegiance to the sage. His primary claim, that he is an unusually perceptive and reliable interpreter, obviously lends itself to creating such credibility because it directs the audience's attention to the center of his enterprise, and when he

---

Eliot, *Felix Holt the Radical* (New York, W. W. Norton, 1970), pp. ix–xxi; Catherine Gallagher, "The Failure of Realism: *Felix Holt,*" *Nineteenth-Century Fiction* 35 (1980): 372–84. Norman Vance, "Law, Religion and the Unity of *Felix Holt,*" in *George Eliot: Centenary Essays and an Unpublished Fragment,* ed. Anne Smith (Totowa, N.J., Barnes & Noble, 1980), writes about the novel as a major success but nonetheless describes its protagonist as "a pillar of uninteresting unrighteousness, with few crucial choices to make and almost nothing important to learn from experience. This makes him useless as a sympathetic unifying focus of the book's personal and social concerns" (119).

[10]Although Barbara Hardy, "The Reticent Narrator," in *Particularities: Readings in George Eliot* (London, Peter Owen, 1982), pp. 126–46, does not concern itself directly with the way Eliot's narrators create credibility, its discussions of the novelist's abandonment of an explicitly male narrator and development of a female one provide valuable materials for a consideration of this topic.

162

can substantiate that claim by revealing unexpected significance in contemporary phenomena, he has won a major part of the battle. Likewise, his word-painting, definition, and creation of effective symbolical grotesques all function to make his pronouncements more credible.

Yet another means of creating ethos, one far more effective with Victorian than with modern readers, appears in the range of biblical echoes, allusion, and patterns of Scripture that characterize many works of the Victorian sage. Such use of biblical texts and standard interpretations of them, particularly in terms of types, colors much Victorian nonfiction, providing imagery, argument, and allusion. Carlyle, Arnold, and Ruskin all make extensive use of such complex echoes of Scripture.[11] In fact, as Susan Hardy Aiken has demonstrated, even unbelievers like John Stuart Mill employed biblical patterns for rhetorical effect.[12] Such allusions to the Bible and to the interpretive traditions by which it was commonly understood play a role in virtually all the sage's other techniques. They appear, for example, throughout various portions of the prophetic pattern, especially in the sage's announcement of his interpretative project and in his visionary close, both of which frequently employ allusions to prophetic texts. Furthermore, although not all symbolical grotesques can accommodate scriptural allusions, those of Carlyle, who often alludes to the brazen serpent and the pillars of cloud and fire, often make elaborate, witty use of them. For example, in constructing a symbolical grotesque from the never-built monument that provides the subject of "Hudson's Statue," he rings many changes on the central conceit that modern worship of commercial success is a poison from which we can be saved only by having the subject of our faith held up before us (as was the brass image of the serpent in Numbers 21:8).[13] Finally, the use of

[11]Paul L. Sawyer, *Ruskin's Poetic Argument: The Design of the Major Works* (Ithaca, Cornell University Press, 1985), pp. 169–70 and 209–20, discusses *The Political Economy of Art* and *Unto This Last*. Landow, *Victorian Types*, pp. 110–14, discusses Ruskin's use of biblical symbolism in *Modern Painters*, *The Seven Lamps of Architecture*, and *The Stones of Venice*; Carlyle's use of political applications of orthodox biblical types is discussed on pp. 166–76.

[12]"Scripture and Poetic Discourse in *The Subjection of Women*," *PMLA* 98 (1985): 353–73.

[13]Landow, *Victorian Types*, pp. 166–76, provides a detailed examination of Car-

tone and technique drawn from contemporary sermons, like the frequent citation of Scripture and commonplace scriptural exegetics, struck just the right note for many portions of the Victorian audience. Carlylean zeal, like that of Ruskin and Thoreau, proved effective here, as on occasion did Arnoldian urbanity.

Certainly, some of the most important techniques for creating ethos are those that involve autobiography and the revelation of intimate experience. The grounding of these techniques in the personal is entirely appropriate, since the ultimate appeal of the sage, to which all of his other techniques contribute, is that his interpretations, criticisms, and suggestions can be believed, finally, because he is a morally and intellectually *trustworthy* person. Anything, therefore, that purports to provide readers with information about the speaker that can convince them either that he possesses admirable intellectual, moral, or other traits or that he speaks from authentic experience makes his statements more acceptable. Such techniques for creating the sage's credibility sometimes involve what purport to be revelations of his most intimate, most private thoughts and experiences. These attempts to *authenticate* the sage—for the sage must be authenticated before his message can be—often involve admissions of major weakness.

Before looking at the more complex strategies involving autobiographical reference, I propose to examine those that function rather more simply as *topoi*, or rhetorical commonplaces, that imply the sage's statements arise in personal experience. In its simplest version this technique takes the form of "Reader, as I was walking down the street, I saw ... " Thus, in "Traffic" Ruskin opens his discussion of class, taste, and national character with such a citation of personal experience. He has already stated a central *sententia* of this lecture: "What we *like* determines what we *are*, and is the sign of what we are; and to teach taste is inevitably to form character" (18.436), and he continues, thereby moving from abstract or generalized statement to an almost casual mention of personal experience:

As I was thinking over this, in walking up Fleet Street the other

---

lyle's manipulation in "Hudson's Statue" of the type of the brazen serpent.

day, my eye caught the title of a book standing open in a booksell-
er's window. It was—"On the necessity of the diffusion of taste
among all classes." "Ah," I thought to myself, "my classifying friend,
when you have diffused your taste, where will your classes be? The
man who likes what you like, belongs to the same class with you, I
think. Inevitably so. You may put him to other work if you choose;
but, by the condition you have brought him into, he will dislike the
work as much as you would yourself. You get hold of a scavenger or
a costermonger, who enjoyed the Newgate Calendar for literature,
and 'Pop goes the Weasel' for music. You think you can make him
like Dante and Beethoven? I wish you joy of your lessons; but if you
do, you have made a gentleman of him:—he won't go back to his
costermongering." (18.436–37)

We have all the usual devices of the sage here vouched for by citation of homely personal experience and the informal, personal
tone with which it is presented: Ruskin has taken his casual encounter with a minor contemporary phenomenon and from it produced a characteristic definition, interpretation, and satiric emblem. Furthermore, like Carlyle's and Arnold's quotation of
newspaper and other reports, this brief personal narrative demonstrates not only that the sage can perceive that such apparently
trivial phenomena have something important to tell us but also
that he can communicate that significance to his audience. One of
the most important aspects of this device for creating ethos is the
very informality and even humility with which it presents the sage.
Since Ruskin, like Carlyle and other nineteenth-century sages, often treats his audience so harshly and with such aggression, these
brief intimate passages do much to soothe the feelings of its members, act as transition between such attacks, or otherwise provide
some relief to the audience. Such personal glimpses of the sage,
which can serve as acts of gracious condescension, also strive to
win favor with the audience by establishing a sense of community
between him and his readers or listeners.

The most important effect of such autobiographical testimony,
however, is that it establishes an authorial persona that the audience can trust. A major source of such techniques is Montaigne,
who continually cites his own experience and character when he
attempts both to tell the entire truth and to win his reader's assent

to it. Part of his reason for telling so much about himself obviously derives from a characteristic skepticism, which distrusts any broad theories and generalizations. He therefore desires to root his ideas in a specific context while also allowing others to perceive possible connections that he himself may have missed. Presenting the context within which his ideas took form, he necessarily must also characterize himself since he constitutes the most important context, and hence he advises his reader: "As my fancies present themselves, I pile them up; now they come pressing in a crowd, now dragging single file. I want people to see my natural and ordinary pace, however off the track it is. I let myself go as I am."[14] Much of the time he simply draws instances from his own experience of himself because, as he points out in "Of Experience," he knows himself better than anyone else. "I study myself more than any other subject. That is my metaphysics, that is my physics" (821).

This belief that one's personal and personally achieved knowledge has more authenticity (and hence credibility) than that acquired from one's community appears in the Victorian emphasis upon autobiography. In fact, what makes autobiography as a mode so characteristic of the age is that it provides a means of finding public uses for private experience and thus answers one of the central Victorian problems. As E. D. H. Johnson has pointed out, the major Victorian authors made heroic attempts to strike a proper balance between the demands of society and of self. In particular, Tennyson, Browning, and Arnold sought "to define the sphere within which the modern poet may exercise his faculty, while holding in legitimate balance the rival claims of his private, aristocratic insights and of the tendencies existing in a society progressively vulgarized by the materialism of the nineteenth and twentieth centuries. Thus it came about that the double awareness, which so generally characterized the Victorian literary mind, grew almost into a perpetual state of consciousness in these poets through their efforts to work out a new aesthetic position for the artist."[15] This "double awareness" derives from (and in turn pro-

---

[14]"Of Books" in *The Complete Essays*, trans. Donald M. Frame (Stanford, Stanford University Press, 1958), p. 297. Hereafter cited in text.

[15]*The Alien Vision of Victorian Poetry: Sources of the Poetic Imagination in Tenny-*

duces) heroic attempts to maintain a hold on both public and private, subjective and objective, feeling and fact. One result of such a double awareness, as David J. DeLaura has pointed out, appears in the way that autobiography pervades Victorian nonfiction: "A great deal of the most notable prose of the century—even whole books-full—consists of 'passages' and highly digressive 'essays'" unified by a "a unique meditative or reflective strain . . . bound together by a continuous, or at least intermittent, readiness for self-exploration and self-manifestation and the manipulation of one's own personal presence for highly diverse ends."[16] Victorian poetry, fiction, painting, and autobiography and other kinds of nonfiction in the period all sought new forms to accommodate private experience, simultaneously making it relevant to the needs of others. Like *Sartor Resartus*, *In Memoriam*, *David Copperfield*, *The Light of the World*, and *Modern Painters*, these nineteenth-century histories of the self find public uses for private experience in forms that at the same time open the self to others and seek some way to protect that fragile individuality from them.

In *Culture and Anarchy* Arnold playfully mocks the characteristic Victorian citation of autobiography when he asserts that nearly every English man and woman contains the elements of Barbarian, Philistine, and Populace. "For instance, I myself (I again take myself as a sort of *corpus vile* to serve for illustration in a matter where serving for illustration may not by every one be thought agreeable), I myself am properly a Philistine,—Mr. Swinburne would add, the son of a Philistine. And although through circumstances which will perhaps one day be known if ever the affecting history of my conversion comes to be written, I have, for the most part, broken with the ideas and the tea-meetings of my own class" (5.144). As Arnold's tongue-in-cheek mention of evangelical conversion narratives suggests, not all sages share intimate personal ex-

---

son, *Browning, and Arnold* (Princeton, Princeton University Press, 1952), p. xiii. See also Masao Miyoshi, *The Divided Self: A Perspective on the Literature of the Victorians* (New York and London, New York University Press, 1969).

[16]"The Allegory of Life: The Autobiographical Impulse in Victorian Prose," *Approaches to Victorian Autobiography*, ed. George P. Landow (Athens, Ohio University Press, 1979), p. 333. See also the chapter entitled "Memory," in John R. Reed, *Victorian Conventions* (Athens, Ohio University Press, 1975).

periences for rhetorical effect. In particular, Carlyle, who remains closer to the pose and tone of the Old Testament prophet than do the others, uses no literal autobiographical examples.

One must also emphasize that however much the sage's citations of autobiographical testimony partake of a characteristic Victorian need, their primary rhetorical purpose is to convince the reader that the author writes from personally achieved experience—and that he therefore writes as an honest, trustworthy man. Indeed, as we see from Montaigne's citations of his own experience, such manner of proceeding inevitably suggests that one speaks about a subject upon which one is an incontrovertible expert at the same time that it implicitly makes the claim that one is an honest, frank, forthright speaker of the truth, above all a *trustworthy* person. Once Montaigne, for example, has demonstrated an expert knowledge of himself, he then claims to be able to extrapolate from it.

> This long attention that I devote to studying myself trains me also to judge passably of others, and there are few things of which I speak more felicitously and excusably.... By training myself from my youth to see my own life mirrored in that of others, I have acquired a studious bent in that subject, and when I am thinking about it, I let few things around me which are useful for that purpose escape my notice: countenances, humors, statements.... The scholars distinguish and mark off their ideas more specifically and in detail. I, who cannot see beyond what I have learned from experience, without any system, present my ideas in a general way, and tentatively. ("Of Experience," 824)

Although Montaigne's Victorian and modern heirs rarely write from such explicitly skeptical premises, some, like Ruskin, Lawrence, Mailer, and Didion, frequently cite autobiography for much the same reason as had their predecessor—to convince their readers by purporting to reveal the surroundings within which an idea took shape. Although the conception of the sage as master of experience does not demand that he write directly from his own experience, many such passages in fact take the form of autobiographical records. For example, we recall that when Ruskin attacks Poussin's *La Riccia* he proceeds by comparing the painting with a word-painting of the scene itself, which he begins by explicitly stating that his knowledge of the actual landscape derives from personal experience: "Not long ago," he informs the reader, "I was slowly descending this very bit of carriage-road, the first turn after you leave Albano" (3.278). Unlike his mention in "Traffic" of his encounter with a book on the diffusion of taste, this citation of personal experience emphasizes, not his intellectual acuity, but his capacity for experience. It also emphasizes, as do most such word-paintings in autobiographical passages, that the writer has a personally achieved, rather than a secondhand, knowledge. Ruskin frequently asserts that he has such personal knowledge, particularly in his earlier writings on art, and whereas his brilliant bird's-eye view of the Mediterranean in *The Stones of Venice* (10.186–87) obviously exemplifies a purely imagined sight, his opening discussions of the doges' tombs (9.48–51), like his tour of Torcello (10.17–19) and the inside of St. Mark's (10.85–89), are presented as the records of personal experience by a master of vision.

This entire matter of citing one's own experiences—or as Arnold puts it so well, using oneself as a *corpus vile*—relates intimately to the common technique of creating *ethos* by confessions of weakness, shortcomings, and error. Once again, Montaigne provides both an example and a source of this means of creating credibility. As many passages in the *Essays* demonstrate, he reveals his most intimate personal habits and preferences, willingly informing the reader of matters generally hidden or ignored. We learn his fears, his preferences in eating and sleeping, the minor details of his health, the frequency and method of his urinating and defecating. Such revelations of private facts are closely related to the common technique used by the sages for which Montaigne also provides major precedent—the creation of ethos by confessing one's shortcomings—for in both cases one attempts to win the audience's credence by sharing details with it that one usually keeps secret. As Emerson points out: "Montaigne is the frankest and honestest of all writers. His French freedom runs into grossness; but he has anticipated all censure by the bounty of his own confessions. . . . nobody can think or say worse of him than he does. . . . But, with all this really superfluous frankness, the opinion of an invincible probity grows into every reader's mind" ("Montaigne; or, the Skep-

169

tic," 698). Emerson's comment is particularly valuable, since it provides evidence of the effect such techniques had upon one nineteenth-century reader.

Montaigne's means of creating this impression of "invincible probity" take many forms, not all of which exemplify authentic revelation or confession. For example, although he accuses himself in "Of the Inconsistency of Our Actions" of a multitude of shortcomings—he is alternately chaste and lascivious, clever and stupid, surly and affable, lying and truthful (242)—such citations of his own flaws hardly constitute his true confessional mode, since he cites himself as a typical instance of flaws and inconsistencies that he believes to be shared by all people. He uses the true confessional mode, however, in "Of Cruelty" when he insists that he is hardly a virtuous man. "I am so far from having arrived at that first and most perfect degree of excellence where virtue becomes a habit," he confesses, "that even of the second degree I have hardly given any proof. I have not put myself to great effort to curb the desires by which I have found myself pressed. My virtue is a virtue, or should I say an innocence, that is accidental and fortuitous" (311). Such confessions urge upon us that the author is frank, sincere, and honest, that one who so willingly reveals his own shortcomings, intellectual, social, and moral, can be trusted to tell the truth.

Paradoxically, both assertions of strength and admissions of weakness can contribute to the sage's credibility. Although Carlyle writes with the extreme confidence of the biblical prophet, Ruskin and Thoreau generally admit weakness or error as a way of winning the audience's allegiance. One clear admission of supposed weakness takes the form of a *topos* we can describe as "Excuse me, friends, because I am being forced to say these painful truths." Thoreau, for instance, opens "A Plea for Captain John Brown" by claiming to have been driven, apparently against his will, to speak on Brown's behalf: "I trust that you will pardon me for being here. I do not wish to force my thoughts upon you, but I feel forced myself. Little as I know of Captain Brown, I would fain do my part to correct the tone and the statements of the newspapers, and of my countrymen generally, respecting his character and actions. It costs us nothing to be just" (111). In response to the disavowals of

Brown by New Englanders after his arrest at Harper's Ferry, Thoreau has himself rung the bell of the Concord, Massachusetts, town hall and read his "Plea" to his assembled fellow citizens; he delivered his defense of Brown a day later in Boston and Worcester. Thoreau in this matter is obviously pursuing an unpopular, even dangerous course, and during the progress of his speech he will savagely ridicule his listeners. He therefore begins by emphasizing in tones of great humility that his actions arise in some way outside himself. He claims that a sense of justice forces him to speak against his will—and by so doing he of course lays claim to a moral stature greater than that of his listeners who have felt no such need to speak the truth or defend a martyr.

Ruskin similarly begins "Traffic," a lecture he delivered at the town hall, Bradford, on 21 April 1864, by protesting to the audience that he has been forced to speak against his will and apologizing to its members for what they will hear. Addressing them as his "good Yorkshire friends," he reminds them that they have invited him to talk about "this Exchange you are going to build: but, earnestly and seriously asking you to pardon me, I am going to do nothing of the kind." Ruskin explains that he can say very little about their exchange because he "must talk of quite other things, though not willingly;—I could not deserve your pardon, if, when you invited me to speak on one subject, I *wilfully* spoke on another" (18.433). Here we encounter the same opening note of apology and the same humility that we find in Thoreau's "A Plea for Captain John Brown." And like Thoreau, Ruskin quickly shifts tone and treats his audience aggressively. In fact, he ends his first paragraph with the candid admission: "I do not *care* about this Exchange of yours," but he then soothes his audience by telling them that he did not wish to be rude by turning down the invitation to speak, after which he tells them he doesn't care about their "Exchange—because *you* don't; and because you know perfectly well I cannot make you" (18.433). One reason, he explains, that they do not concern themselves earnestly with the architecture for the exchange is that it does not cost very much. According to him, the cost of such an exchange is to them, collectively, nothing, and in fact buying a new coat is a more important financial outlay to him than erecting this planned building is to them. "But you think you may as well have the right thing for your money. You know there are a great many odd styles of architecture about; you don't want to do anything ridiculous; you hear of me, among others, as a respectable architectural man-milliner; and you send for me, that I may tell you the leading fashion; and what is, in our shops, for the moment, the newest and sweetest thing in pinnacles" (18.434). By reducing his enterprise as a critic of architecture to the level of millinery, he mocks himself for receiving so little of his audience's respect, and in this way he makes some small amends for the abrasive charge that it cares little about the proposed subject of his talk. But, of course, drawing such an analogy between himself and the female milliner not only points out how little respect his listeners have for him as man and thinker, it tells far more harshly upon them, since the analogy implies that they perceive little more in a matter crucial to their society than transitory fashion. (Paradoxically, like many satirical analogies that cut at least two ways, this one begins to take on an unexpected validity by the close of the lecture, for as the audience gradually realizes that architecture does indeed clothe and body forth a nation's inner self, one also perceives that Ruskin's initial satire has a Carlylean application and truth. Like Carlyle's Teufelsdröckh, Ruskin has shown that buildings are in a sense clothes, symbols of spiritual facts that they embody.)

Likewise, Ruskin's extensive commentary on his former views and mistakes in the footnotes to later editions of *Modern Painters* is also a device to create ethos; it convinces the reader of his openness and willingness to admit error—and hence guarantees the authenticity of his present views. Such self-deprecation often appears near the beginning of a work in this form. Ruskin's admission in "Traffic" that most members of his audience consider him little more than a man-milliner and Arnold's in *Culture and Anarchy* that he is a product of the aggressively uncultured middle classes cultivate their audiences' sympathy.

Ethos as "Plot" in Writings of the Sage

One of the prime distinctions between the earlier sages and

those of the past decades lies in the fact that writers of the late twentieth century not only present themselves in terms of a far less elevated, less magisterial persona than had their predecessors but also urge upon their readers their own flaws and weaknesses to an unprecedented degree. Like Montaigne, Didion and Mailer tell us about their basic, perhaps their innermost attitudes and habits of mind as if it were necessary to know these facts about them before we could appreciate the authenticity of their writings. In Didion and Mailer as in Montaigne such willingness to thrust the author's own qualities forward has several sources. First, an essential skepticism and consequent relativism require that, to tell the reader the truth as they see it, they reveal the habits of mind and attitudes within which these ideas arose. They choose such a tack, it appears, because they suspect that their ideas might be genetically related to such mental geography, and to be honest they must therefore permit their audience to draw its own conclusions. Then, of course, such essentially confessional modes—even when the confessions involve matters of intellect and not sin or flaw—have a rhetorical intention as they always have a rhetorical effect, for as we have already seen, such admissions always implicitly claim that the author has so freely confessed his or her own weaknesses that we the audience can trust everything that follows. I do not know how one can accurately determine the relative weight of these two intentions, but given the obvious fact the writings of the sage depend so heavily upon convincing the sage's audience that he deserves credence, I suspect that the rhetorical takes precedence over the confessional one.

At its simplest, such an admission can take the form of presenting the author's surroundings as she writes, something Didion does in the opening of "On Morality:" "As it happens I am in Death Valley, in a room at the Enterprise Motel and Trailer Park, and it is July, and it is hot. In fact it is 119. I cannot seem to make the air conditioner work, but there is a small refrigerator, and I can wrap ice cubes in a towel and hold them against the small of my back. With the help of the ice cubes I have been trying to think, because *The American Scholar* asked me to, in some abstract way about 'morality,' a word I distrust more every day, but my mind veers inflexibly toward the particular" (*Slouching towards Bethlehem*,

157). Didion continues by mentioning the particulars of an automobile accident nearby and then shows how they contain information about morality, her stated subject. The point is that she begins by revealing the physical and psychological setting within which she writes. She claims in this way to tell the truth, the whole truth.

A related means of supplying the context of one's own ideas involves presenting a thumbnail self-portrait that purports to provide a frank survey of one's essential qualities. Didion's "In the Islands" makes use of this technique, familiar since Montaigne, of informing the reader about the author's strengths and weaknesses, likes and dislikes, to provide a sense of context for her ideas. After narrating how she, her husband, and her daughter sit in their Honolulu hotel and wait for news of an expected tidal wave, she adds that she has come to Hawaii instead of filing for divorce, after which she explains that she has related these intimate facts "because I want you to know, as you read me, precisely who I am and where I am and what is on my mind. I want you to understand exactly what you are getting" (*White Album*, 133).

Like Mailer, who begins by presenting his own shortcomings as a reporter, Didion frankly, almost aggressively, thrusts her potential shortcomings as a truth-teller upon the reader. The weaknesses each chooses to exploit, however, suggest what differentiates male and female applications of the sage's ethos—and what, therefore, can differentiate the works of men and women who write as sages. In "Letter from Paradise," which contains her poignant ruminations upon Hawaii as a place of loss, Didion admits to such extreme emotionality (conventionally, if not in reality, a woman's weakness) that she cannot observe what she has come to report. The occasion is her trip on one of the bright pink tour boats that take the visitor to the sites of several sunken warships that still lie in Pearl Harbor. After describing the way the tour begins in a "kind of sleazy festivity," she mentions that at first amid such surroundings "it is hard to remember what we came to remember."

> And then something happens. I took that bright pink boat to
> Pearl Harbor on two afternoons, but I still do not know what I went
> to find out, which is how other people respond a quarter of a cen-

Another main version of this basic technique for creating ethos, of which Didion also provides a modern example, emphasizes intellectual rather than emotional weakness. Again, the often detailed presentation required to turn such admissions of flaws into strengths permits (and occasionally forces) the writer into making it the central structure of a work. For instance, "On Keeping a Notebook," which employs this version of the confessional mode, begins by advising the reader that Didion has never kept one "to have an accurate factual record of what I have been doing or thinking" because that would require "an instinct for reality which I sometimes envy but do not possess" (*Slouching towards Bethlehem*, 133). Once again, what begins as a confession of weakness is intended to end up implying strength. Didion's subsequent confession that she has trouble retaining facts and also lives in a slovenly manner quickly transforms itself into a claim that she deals instead with higher imaginative truths. Thus her notebook, which contains bits and snippets of overheard conversations, eccentrically observed phenomena, and other apparently trivial facts, turns out—are we surprised?—to justify her claims to high intellect and imagination: "What is a recipe for sauerkraut doing in my notebook? What kind of magpie keeps this notebook? '*He was born the night the Titanic went down.*' That seems a nice enough line, and I even recall who said it, but is it not really a better line in life than it could ever be in fiction?" (138). In fact, that is exactly the point of her notebook entries—not that they provide data upon which to base her writings but rather that they provide tags, brief spots of time, that allow her to retrieve her past and hence be a coherent human being. After claiming that "it all comes back" to her, she explains that this ability to maintain contact with one's past selves is absolutely necessary. "I think we are well advised to keep on nodding terms with the people we used to be, whether we find them attractive company or not. Otherwise they turn up unannounced and surprise us, come hammering on the mind's door at 4 a.m. of a bad night and demand to know who deserted them, who betrayed them, who is going to make amends" (139). Such assertions of her own ability to retrieve her past from such fragments of language and image both authenticate her claims to know herself, her claims to ruthless honesty, and also demonstrate her courage and wisdom. To her it all comes back, Didion tells us. Even an old sauerkraut recipe bears significance since it dates back to a time, a particular night, she wishes to preserve: "I was on Fire Island when I first made that sauerkraut, and it was raining, and we drank a lot of bourbon and ate the sauerkraut and went to bed at ten, and I listened to the rain and the Atlantic and felt safe" (141). Like Ruskin's quoting in *Modern Painters* and *Fors Clavigera* from diaries and letters written years and even decades earlier, Didion's public examination of her notebooks goes far to establishing her claims as a truth-teller. Here is a person, we are supposed to realize, who cares about getting it right, a person who wants to know the truth about herself. Here is a person, so goes the implicit claim, whom we can *trust*. In addition, such citation of autobiographical data not only demonstrates the writer's sincerity, openness, and courageous honesty, it also demonstrates Didion's ability at interpretation and retrieval.[17] Like Newman, Ruskin, Lawrence, and others who make frequent use of such autobiographical data, Didion commits us to a literature of experience and lends us her own memories and experiences.

The White Album, Didion's collage of Californian images from the late 1960s, exemplifies her most important and most successful use of autobiographical data in such a literature of experience. From the point of view of one studying the modern sage's attempts to create ethos, *The White Album* also exemplifies perhaps her most important use of intellectual weakness both to claim intellectual strength and to make the points that claim ultimately supports. Such thematized technique makes its appearance in the opening paragraphs when she tells us, "I am talking here about a time when I began to doubt the premises of all the stories I had ever told myself, a common condition but one I found troubling" (*White Album*, 11). As it turns out, then, Didion has chosen these images because for her they capture the experiences of 1966–71, which she takes to be a crucial turning point in the life of herself and her time. Like Ruskin, Carlyle, Newman, and a host of nine-

---

[17]Howard M. Helsinger, "Credence and Credibility: The Concern for Honesty in Victorian Autobiography," in *Approaches to Victorian Autobiography*, pp. 39–63, provides an excellent discussion of the autobiographer's means of winning his audience's trust.

teenth-century predecessors, Didion as sage elects to make a crisis, a crisis survived, the test case by which she can explain—impose another story upon—events for the sake of her reader. Taking herself as paradigm like Newman and these other writers of what have come to be termed "conversion narratives," Didion offers her own experience as a Sign of the Times.[18] These are the events, she tells us, that puzzled her. These are the events for which she could not find or invent the "right" story.

In the manner consecrated by so many Victorians, she presents her crisis as significant, as immediately relevant, to us. Unlike Carlyle or Ruskin, she does not, however, use biblical imagery to suggest the archetypal nature of her experience, for unlike them, although she may perceive herself in an all too common situation, she finds no solace, no *usefulness*, in figuring herself forth as an Ishmael, as an Israelite wandering in the desert, or as a person trying to gain admission to the ark.[19] In her words, such analogies are not "workable"; they do not explain anything any longer. She was able to exist, to survive, during these years, and indeed she gave

> an adequate enough performance, as improvisations go. The only problem was that my entire education, everything I have ever been told or told myself, insisted that the production was never meant to be improvised: I was supposed to have a script, and had mislaid it. I was supposed to hear cues, and no longer did. I was meant to know

[18]Such retailings of one's own experience as paradigm for others goes back at least as far as the *Confessions* of St. Augustine and the *Golden Ass* of Apuleius. For the origins, in England, of such conversion narratives, see Paul Delany, *British Autobiography in the Seventeenth Century* (London, Routledge & Kegan Paul, 1969). See also John N. Morris, *Versions of the Self* (New York, Basic Books, 1966).

[19]For two important studies of Victorian use of analogies and orthodox biblical types in autobiography, see Avrom Fleishman, "Personal Myth: Three Victorian Autobiographers," and Linda H. Peterson, "Biblical Typology and the Self-Portrait of the Poet in Robert Browning," both in *Approaches to Victorian Autobiography*, pp. 215–34 and 235–68. See also Avrom Fleishman, *Figures of Autobiography: The Language of Self-Writing in Victorian and Modern England* (Berkeley, University of California Press, 1983). Barbara K. Lewalski, "Typological Symbolism and the 'Progress of the Soul' in Seventeenth-Century Literature," in *Literary Uses of Typology from the Middle Ages to the Present*, ed. Earl Miner (Princeton, Princeton University Press, 1977), pp. 79–114, contains essential background for the history of what she calls "correlative types."

the plot, but all I knew was what I saw: flash pictures in variable sequence, images with no "meaning" beyond their temporary arrangement, not a movie but a cutting-room experience. In what would probably be the middle of my life I wanted still to believe in the narrative and in the narrative's intelligibility, but to know that one could change the sense with every cut was to begin to perceive the experience as rather more electrical than ethical. (*White Album*, 12–13)

Having begun her personal album of the late sixties with a gathering of puzzling images, she now presents a puzzling one that horrifies us—the image of a child purposely abandoned to die on the divider of a California highway. The problem for her, for us: "Certain of these images did not fit into any narrative I knew" (13).

Didion's somewhat reduced version of prophetic stature retains many of the Victorian sage's claims and characteristics. Like Carlyle and Thoreau, she writes both as one who is an outsider and as one who has much in common with the audience. Furthermore, she establishes her claims to credibility in part by an astute alternation of satire and sympathy that tends to create the sense of a superior intellect and moral sense judiciously assigning praise and blame. Again, the act of making an unexpected interpretation and an unexpected discovery of relevance establishes ethos. Unlike the earlier sages, Didion achieves these effects in part by making specific, detailed admissions of weakness, and her weakness turns out to be at least a partial strength, or strength within a particular context, because only such a sense of dread would have led to her recognitions.

Mailer's *Of a Fire on the Moon* similarly thrusts his egotism, self-display, and other shortcomings upon the reader as a means both of assuring that reader about his essential honesty and also of revealing unexpected strengths. Like Didion, he uses the more elaborate forms of creating authorial credibility to provide a center to his entire investigative enterprise. Employing a literary strategy important at least since *The Prelude* and *In Memoriam*, these authors make themselves paradigms, Every(wo)men, whose admissions of weakness and experiences of crisis not only serve as Signs of the

179

Times but also lead to important means for their readers to understand themselves and the age. These attempts to create ethos, in other words, serve as thematic centers, concentrations of techniques that convey the author's ideas and ideology. More than that, they provide the reader of this kind of prose with a means of reading, with a way to follow the "plot" (for, in fact, the twists and turns of authorial attempts to produce credibility provide a nonfictional analogue to the plot of fictional narrative). These various moves and strategies that the sage employs to create ethos provide a set of signals to the reader, which in turn provide clues to how the work is to be read.

Such a strong, intrusive authorial persona does, however, involve major rhetorical risks. Tom Wolfe's writing, which avoids both such a self-conscious use of this kind of persona and the risks it can produce, points up the importance of ethos in this genre. In particular, although Wolfe's dispersion of the author's presence into different voices avoids many of the rhetorical difficulties created by sages such as Ruskin and Mailer who thrust themselves into our notice, it frequently creates other major problems, not all of which he manages to solve. His floating point of view and multiple voices succeed in conveying the attitudes and experience of many of his subjects, but nevertheless, the impression of sympathy his techniques convey creates serious, sometimes insoluble, rhetorical difficulties in his satirical pieces. Because these sketches, which are essentially latter-day versions of Carlyle's *Latter-Day Pamphlets*, always take a particularly mordant view of their subjects, whether mod office boys in "The Noonday Underground" or rising executives in "The Mid-Atlantic Man," Wolfe's reliance upon entering the satirized figure's imaginative world often strikes the reader—at least this reader—as betrayal of these figures and hence morally suspect. Wolfe's turning to attack a character on whom he has lavished so much sympathy comes across as cruel and inhumane—and hence does much to undermine his credibility.

Another related source of rhetorical (and moral) difficulties lies in Wolfe's emphasis upon problems of status throughout many of these satirical pieces, for after taking his reader into what he terms the "statusphere" of his characters, he always ends up demonstrating how the subcultures they inhabit never truly function as independently as they seem to do to their inhabitants, and as they first seemed to do when Wolfe showed them to us. In every case society, the establishment, or whatever one wishes to call it has the final word, and the English adolescents in their noonday underground, the American ones at a California beach, and all of his other specimens always turn out to be poor, deluded, powerless fools. Despite their novelty and often original vantage points, these satiric pieces turn out to be conservative, even reactionary, because they all imply that the old social order still is not only dominant but the only correct standard. Such a conclusion coming after such apparently daring sympathy with the weird and novel, particularly when combined with Wolfe's entrance into these figures' imaginative worlds, strikes the reader as unsavory because dishonest. Two kinds of work, however, do not fall prey to these problems, those rare pieces, such as "The Truest Sport," in which the tone is not primarily satirical, and those, such as "The Put-Together Girl," in which the target of satire is not the focus of the work.

"A Loss of Ego," the chapter that opens *Of a Fire on the Moon*, repeatedly presents Mailer at his most annoying, and if we can understand how his various statements, admissions, and verbal gestures are intended to act upon the reader, we can better understand and evaluate the work. To begin with, he certainly opens on an odd note. This purported study of the Apollo-Saturn project first presents, not some cultural, technological, or other historical background, but the occasion upon which Mailer heard of Hemingway's death some eight years before, something that the reader might well take at first to be completely irrelevant, a mere bit of self-indulgent rambling. But of course, like Ruskin's initial announcements in "Traffic" that he cannot meet his audience's needs and expectations, it proves to be nothing of the sort. First of all, it permits Mailer to warn the reader about his strengths and weaknesses as a reporter and as one who reacts to contemporary events. Mailer admits (in the book's second paragraph): "Of course, he finally gave a statement. His fury that the world was not run so well as he could run it encouraged him to speak. The world could always learn from what he had to say—his confidence was built on just so hard a diamond" (3). His willing admissions of

181

such egotism and his following admissions of "gracelessly" inveighing "how the death would put secret cheer in every bureaucrat's heart" (4) suggest how frankly he will treat his reader, and he soon explains the relevance of Hemingway's death to the Apollo-Saturn project: "Hemingway constituted the walls of the fort: Hemingway had given the power to believe you could still shout down the corridor of the hospital, live next to the breath of the beast, accept your portion of dread each day. Now the greatest living romantic was dead.... Technology would fill the pause" (4). Hemingway's conception of masculine romance and masculine heroism had provided a spiritual center for Mailer, and when he died it seemed that modern technologies, which permitted no place for the human and no place for heroism, would empty the world of meaning and value. The moon project, the incarnation of the feared technology, forces Mailer to confront that central question, Can heroism, can true humanity, exist within such a technologically oriented endeavor? Or, as he states it much later in the book—"Heroism cohabited with technology. Was the Space Program admirable or abominable? Did God voyage out for NASA, or was the Devil our line of sight to the stars?" (80). "Was the voyage of Apollo 11 the noblest expression of a technological age, or the best evidence of its utter insanity?" (382). Again, like the aggressive opening of Ruskin's "Traffic," Mailer's initial denial of audience expectations turns out to be simultaneously a correction of them and an answer to them.

In the course of announcing his own interpretative project, which is "to comprehend the astronauts" (4), he both explains why he, Norman Mailer, has undertaken such a project and sets forth the strengths and weaknesses that will assist or hinder his succeeding with it. His first strength, says Mailer, is that "he is a detective of sorts, and different in spirit from eight years ago. He has learned to live with questions" (4). Claiming no particular brilliance or even expertise, he characterizes himself as an outsider who is little more than a mediocre reporter. Before long each of these self-criticisms turns out to be an authentication, a certification for his interpretative project. Thus, although he "feels in fact little more than a decent spirit, somewhat shunted to the side," it is the "best possible position for detective work" (4). Similarly, his quixotically unsuccessful campaign for the office of mayor of New York left him "with a huge boredom about himself. He was weary of his own voice, own face, person, persona, will, ideas, speeches, and general sense of importance. He felt not unhappy, mildly depressed, somewhat used up, wise, tolerant, sad, void of vanity, even had a hint of humility" (5–6), and although this self-appraisal, which includes a large dose of self-mockery, obviously presents a markedly unimpressive, rather ordinary, middle-aged version of Mailer, it effectively separates him from his well-known abrasively egotistical, assertive self while suggesting that "detached this season from the imperial demands of his ego" (6), he found himself in the perfect position for such a task as he has proposed.

Even Mailer's denials that he possesses the requirements of a first-rate journalist are intended to elevate him in the reader's estimation. "People he had never met were forever declaring in print that he was the best journalist in America. He thought it was the superb irony of his professional life, for he knew he was not even a good journalist and possibly could not hold a top job if he had to turn in a story every day" (7). He admits, further, that he does not have the consistency, the enormous curiosity, or the drive necessary to be a really good journalist. Such denials obviously permit him to mention the status he has in the eyes of others, thereby providing him with a kind of credential for his enterprise. More important, he is finally able to prove to himself (and to the audience that is always watching his struggles) that orthodox journalism remains inadequate to embrace such phenomena as he encounters. A new method becomes necessary, and he can offer it.

However crucial his possession of certain basic techniques and attitudes necessary to his monumental task, he nonetheless continually strives to create ethos by admitting—indeed by emphasizing—his own flaws and mistakes. He successfully dramatizes his experience of slowly comprehending the nature of the entire project by willingly admitting his errors and narrowness of sympathy. For example, entering the gigantic Vehicle Assembly Building with its forty-story doors, he finds his preconceptions about the joylessness of working with technology incorrect. "He was now forced to recognize the ruddy good cheer and sense of extraordinary morale of the workers in the VAB. As they passed him in the elevators, or

183

as he went by them in the halls and the aisles, a sense of coopera-
tive effort, of absorption in work at hand, and anticipation of the
launch was in the pleasure of their faces. He had never seen an
army of factory workers who looked so happy. . . . Trade-union
geezers, age of fifty, with round faces and silver-rimmed spectacles
strutted like first sergeants at the gate for a three-day pass" (56).
The result of such recognition, Mailer informs us, is that he began
to live "without his ego, a modest quiet observer who went on
trips through the Space Center and took in interviews, and read
pieces of literature connected to the subject, and spent lonely
nights not drinking in his air-conditioned motel room, and
thought—not of himself but of the size of the feat and the project
before him. . . . He was there now merely to observe, to witness"
(56–57). As we encounter Mailer making erroneous judgments and
then correcting them, admitting them to be little more than the
prejudices of the modern liberal intelligentsia and the cultural establishment, we are supposed to credit him with many things: a
flexibility of intellect that permits him to abandon false judgments,
no matter how long or firmly held; a courage to admit his errors
and prejudices even though such admission might make him
appear foolish; a commitment to the truth that makes that truth
appear more important than any need to gain credit for himself.
And, of course, as he changes his opinion, he changes ours as
well.

Throughout *Of a Fire on the Moon* Mailer makes major use of
this confessional mode. For example, before brilliantly narrating
the liftoff, he admits not only to the difficulty he is having getting
any sense of the events about which he plans to write but also to
sheer, banal envy. Thus he explains that he "felt somehow
deprived that he could feel so little. . . . The damn astronauts wer-
en't even real to him" (96), and then he realizes why he finds himself so out of sorts and so annoyed by every little thing and why he
could feel so small. "It was simple masculine envy. He too wanted
to go up in the bird" (97). And when the launch comes, as we
have seen, he has worked hard to become a perfect reporter, who
has earned our credence by admitting so many flaws and shortcomings. His maneuvering to create this effect of trustworthiness appears again in his admission of mixed motives, some good and

some not, when he considers taking a closer look at all the celebrities and politicians who have come to observe the liftoff but then decides that "his liver will simply not permit it. He is here to see the rocket go up, not to stand and look at Very Important People and take notes in a notebook while he sweats in the heat. No, some sense of his own desire to dwell near the rocket, to contemplate its existence as it ascends, and certainly some sense of his own privacy, some demand of his vanity—aware of how grubby he looks and feels—now bids him stay with his own sweaty grubs, the Press and photographers" (90–91). After claiming that he, unlike some other reporters, knows where the important truths of this story lie, Mailer characteristically admits his own vanity as well, as if to reassure us once again that he will tell the whole truth and nothing but the truth, no matter how embarrassing to him.

All these admissions of his own shortcomings, like his brilliant technical analyses and experiential narratives, build toward the ideological climax of the book, which demonstrates that the highest heroism still exists in the midst of the machine. The chief source of Mailer's original fear of technology lay in his suspicion that it removed all risk and opportunity for decision from important endeavors, such as this flight to the moon. The machine, he feared, destroyed individual responsibility by taking away the human capacity to make choices and thereby determine one's fate. In looking into the technology involved in getting men to the moon and returning them safely, he quickly discovers that all those redundancies and redoubled safety systems still cannot remove risk. No matter how many precautions the engineers take, the astronauts' ride on a forty-story bomb involves enormous risk and requires courage, skill, and trust. Moreover, no matter how powerful the computers that their designers produce to assist this lunar and perhaps lunatic enterprise, the men who peer at their screens have to make the crucial decisions. As Mailer reveals in a superbly narrated chapter, "The Ride Down," human beings always need more than the machine can provide, and having stretched it to its capacities, indeed to its breaking point, they must leap into darkness. In fact, the more Mailer looks into the details of the intricate technology, the more he discovers that he has encountered an enterprise he likes, an enterprise at the edge, one that pushes

185

human capacities and demands accepting reponsibility for oneself and others.

The descent of the lunar module to the moon's surface exemplifies the difficulties of the entire mission. The tiny space ship carries little fuel, and those who fly it down to the lunar surface must survive two opposing difficulties: If in the attempt to save fuel they descend too quickly, they will crash the module and die on the surface; if they descend too cautiously, they will use up so much fuel that they will be unable to return to space and will hence also die on the surface. To reduce risk of either eventuality, computers monitor the rate at which fuel is consumed and report the results to Mission Control back on earth. The only problem is that computers cannot always handle their job, and then people have to step in and make quick decisions that determine the survival of two human beings and the fate of a multibillion dollar project. The crisis occurs at the worst possible moment—as the tiny module descends toward the surface. Aldrin radios to Mission Control, "1202," a code that indicates the on-board computer has found itself overloaded and unable to carry out its functions. "In such a case the computer stops, then starts over again. It has recalculated its resources. Now it will take on only the most important functions, drop off the others" (376). Those at Mission Control immediately recognize the gravity of the crisis, because they realize "that if 1202 keeps blinking, the activities of the computer will soon deteriorate. The automatic pilot will first be lost, then control over the thrust of the engine, then Navigation and Guidance—the pilots will have to abort. In fifteen seconds it can all happen" (376–77). Lying upon his back a few feet above the rocket flames as he and his companion hurtle toward the moon's surface, Aldrin asks men a quarter of a million miles away to gauge the seriousness of the problem. Thirty seconds later, after conferring with his staff, Duke Kranz, the Flight Director, decides that the risk indicated by that 1202 is low enough to permit the men to risk landing on the moon.

> Kranz has been quizzing his Guidance officers and his Flight Dynamics officers. It is a ten-second roll call, and each one he queries says GO. The words come in, "GO. GO. GO. GO." The key word

is from Guidance Officer Stephen G. Bales. It is on his console that the 1202 is also blinking. But they have been over the permissible rate of alarm on which they can continue to fly a mission, and the 1202 is not coming in that fast—the Executive Overflow is not constant. So Bales' voice rings out GO. Listening to it on a tape recorder later, there is something like fear in the voice, it is high-pitched, but it rings out. In the thirty seconds between Aldrin's request for a reading and the reply that they were GO, the decision has been taken. (377)

A capacity for major heroism turns out to exist not only in the astronauts, in whom one naturally might expect to find it, but also in those computer jockeys with their crew cuts and short white-sleeved shirts whom Mailer and his friends in the liberal intelligentsia hold in such low regard. Earlier in *Of a Fire on the Moon* he admits that he had trained as an engineer but abandoned engineering to become a writer. The book opens with a Mailer overtly hostile to technology and those who serve it. A confirmed humanist, he fears the destructive effects of technology upon our lives and spirits, and he particularly distrusts scientists, engineers, technocrats, and all other acolytes of the machine. Therefore his climactic recognition that such men have both the capacity and the opportunity to achieve heroism equal to that of Hemingway's bullfighters represents a powerful affirmation to all his questions about the triumph of the human over the mechanical. It further represents Mailer's reconciliation with the ghosts of his own past and his gracious admission that some of those men whom he had long scorned engage in the same endeavors that concern him and concerned Hemingway. Essentially, Mailer demonstrates the role of the machine in culture, as he understands that Arnoldian term.

Mailer's *Of a Fire on the Moon* proves a fitting work with which to end our consideration of this genre, to which he is a late and often brilliant contributor. Like its Victorian antecedents, *Of a Fire on the Moon* emphasizes the sage's definitions and his interpretations of often trivial grotesque phenomena, and like them, it also relies upon an episodic structure that incorporates segments that alternate between satirical attack and positive vision. Like the works of Ruskin, Lawrence, and Wolfe, it presents its author as a master

187

of experience who lends us his feelings and imagination so we can fully perceive some physical fact. Like works of Ruskin, Didion, and others, *Of a Fire on the Moon* also presents its author narrating the experience of interpretation or understanding physical and other facts. Finally, like those of all other works in this genre, its techniques contribute to the creation of authorial ethos, for we finally understand and accept what Mailer has to say because he repeatedly shows us that his methods, his poses, his ideas are necessary.

Afterword

If readers of this book find that it has provided them with a useful way to tackle the works it discusses or that it has enabled them to perceive new connections that join various works of nonfiction, it has succeeded. I am not particularly concerned, therefore, whether readers decide finally that it describes a genre to which both Victorians and moderns have contributed or whether they conclude that Ruskin and Didion, say, work in different, if related, forms. What I am concerned about is to convince the reader that a taxonomy of the kind I have attempted provides a useful approach to understanding nonfiction, for I believe that until teachers and students have an appropriate vocabulary and intellectual organization for classifying literary differences, they are unlikely to perceive them.

Where should we go next? What questions does such a generic description suggest that we ask next? I can think of several, and I expect readers can think of others. First of all, since this genre builds so much upon both Old Testament prophecy and its conventional nineteenth-century readings, one would like to know more about these subjects. One would like to know, in particular, to what extent individual prophetic books had special impact on Victorian authors, and one would also like to determine if any of the prophets had separate or unusual associations connected with them.

Second, one needs more evidence of reader response, particularly reader recognition of the individual techniques of the sage. Those remarks by contemporaries of Carlyle and Arnold with which I opened this book exemplify such needed evidence of contemporary response, more of which I expect can be found in reviews, longer critical consideration, and private correspondence.

A third subject for investigation involves locating those, particularly women, who might have contributed to this genre but whose work has thus far gone unrecognized or has been forgotten. One fairly common contemporary assumption is that since the Victorian prophets wrote in an explicitly public mode, women, who generally found themselves restricted to private ones, such as letters and diaries, never contributed to it in the nineteenth century.[1] Although such a position (which tends to support granting new importance to what are usually considered minor literary modes like letters) has certain obvious appeals, it also has the unfortunate effect of forestalling serious investigation of the question whether women did contribute to this and other public modes of nonfiction. Some evidence suggests that they did. Florence Nightingale's *Cassandra* (1852), which I encountered only after this book was almost completed, certainly has much in common with the more polemical work of Carlyle and Arnold. And there may be many more such works addressed to women that remain unknown to most students of the period. A second reason for hesitating to endorse the notion that women could not have contributed to public modes lies in the conditions of Victorian authorship, much of which was anonymous or eponymous. Since such a large portion of periodical essays appeared without indications of authorship, women had the opportunity to publish on supposedly male subjects in periodicals supposedly directed at men—and Mary Ann Evans was clearly not the only woman to take advantage of this means of publication.[2]

[1]This position was advanced, for example, by several participants in a 1984 Modern Language Association section on the teaching of Victorian nonfiction.
[2]See, for example, Martha Westwater, *The Wilson Sisters: A Biographical Study of Upper Middle-Class Victorian Life* (Athens, Ohio University Press, 1984), which

190

Third, testing the applicability of this kind of generic description to French, German, and other authors who do not participate directly in the Anglo-American tradition might be useful. These explorations might show that the genre has a wider application than I have demonstrated thus far. On the contrary, it might reveal both that it has no contributors writing in languages other than English and why that has been the case.

Finally, one might also wish to investigate those literary intonations, such as parody, that often appear after a form reaches maturity. Oscar Wilde's "The Soul of Man under Socialism" and "The Decay of Lying," like some of Max Beerbohm's essays, appear to have developed as parodies and inversions of, and confrontations with, the writings of the sage. The flippant, witty tone of Wilde and Beerbohm, for instance, which so obviously responds to the Carlylean and Ruskinian sense of the importance of being earnest, also works to create a different kind of ethos, and in this sense confronts the creators of this form. Similarly, when placed in this context, the witty epigrams of Wilde reveal that they act as equivalents to the sage's interpretive set pieces. The entire pose of the aesthete, one may add, shares a surprising amount with that of the secular prophet, for both aesthete and sage position themselves outside the mainstream and accept eccentricity and alienation as the cost of superiority. The sage, in other words, may have strange progeny or stepchildren, and one cannot fully appreciate the importance of the works in this genre until one tracks them all down and discovers all the ways in which the words of these elegant Jeremiahs take form and the possibly strange and unexpected effects they produce.

---

mentions instances of women publishing in *The Economist* and other leading intellectual periodicals.

Index

Index

Brown, John, 64–65, 69
Browning, Elizabeth Barrett, 68
Browning, Robert, 166
Brumm, Ursula, 28n
Buell, Lawrence, 32 + n, 33
Burke, Edmund, 118
Byron, George Gordon, Lord, 100

Capote, Truman, 83
captains of industry, 67n
Carlyle, Thomas, 17, 19, 27, 30, 34,
    35, 40, 47, 49, 58, 59, 60, 69, 72,
    76, 82, 100–1, 104, 110, 112, 114,
    128–29, 156, 162–65, 179, 190;
    influenced Arnold, 70–71 + n;
    influenced Ruskin, 37, 38n, 71,
    96n; influenced Thoreau, 37
    Writings: *Chartism*, 33, 41, 43, 67,
        92, 162; *French Revolution, The*,
        75; "Hudson's Statue," 105;
        Latter-Day Pamphlets, 33, 105,
        180; *On Heroes and
        Hero-Worship*, 67n; *Past and
        Present*, 20, 27, 33, 42, 60n, 61,
        67 + n, 73–74, 82–83, 85–87,
        92–95, 96n, 118; *Sartor Resartus*,
        67n, 118, 167, 172; "Signs of
        the Times," 21, 29n, 33, 61,
        71n
Carpenter, Mary W., 28n
Carson, Herbert L., 56n
Cassian, 37
Catullus, 37
Chatman, Seymour, 155–56n
Cioran, E. M., 40
Coleridge, Samuel Taylor, 23–24, 118
confessions of weakness, 169–72
Coombs, James H., 29 + n
Coulling, Sidney, 98n
Croce, Benedetto, 97
Crummell, Alexander, 67
Curtius, Ernst, 37n

Daily Telegraph, The, 17
Daniels, Mary L., 159n
Dante Alighieri, 37n, 165
definition: Arnold's, 121–23, 128;
    blends theme and technique,
    127–31; Carlyle's, 118–19;
    corrective, 128; and homiletic
    tradition, 117–18; implications of,
    116; Ruskin's, 119–20, 126–27;
    satiric use of, 123–27; sources of
    technique, 117–18; Thoreau's use
    of, 120–21, 124–26, 178n
Delaney, Paul, 72n
DeLaura, David J., 37, 71n, 98n, 167
Dennis, George, 141n
Dickens, Charles, 156–57 + n, 167
Didion, Joan, 20, 21, 72, 75, 83,
    104, 189; draws upon Ruskin,
    37 + n
    Writings: "Comrade Laski C. P. U.
        S. A. (M.-L.)," 105n; "In the
        Islands," 174; "James Pike,"
        104–5; "Letter from Paradise,"
        174–75; "On Keeping a
        Notebook," 176–77; "On
        Morality," 173; "Seacoast of
        Despair, The," 105–6; "7000
        Romaine, Los Angeles 38,"
        105n; *Slouching towards
        Bethlehem*, 34, 105, 128; *White
        Album, The*, 34, 46–49, 60,
        177–79
discontinuous literary structure, 27,
    97–98
Disraeli, Benjamin, 19, 20
Doda, Carol, 107–12, 114
Dryden, John, 20
Du Bois, William Edward Burghardt,
    66–67 + n
Du Fresnoy, Charles A., 20
Dumas, Alexandre, 66
Dürer, Albrecht, 82

194

Index

Keller, Karl, 28n
Kerrigan, William, 29n
Kingsley, Charles, 25, 117–18
Kirkpatrick, A. F., 26n

Lamb, Charles, 133
Landow, George P., 28n, 32n, 37n, 67n, 71n, 79n, 134n, 158n
Lane, Lauriat, 56n
LaValley, Albert J., 19
Lawrence, D. H., 49, 72, 132, 146, 152, 168, 177, 187
  Writings: *Etruscan Places*, 34; *Fantasia of the Unconscious, The*, 34; *Sea and Sardinia*, 34, 89, 141–42; *Twilight in Italy*, 34, 139–42
Levine, George, 19, 161–62n
Lewalski, Barbara K., 178n
Lisbon earthquake, 43n
Longinus, 74
Lorraine, Claude, 135
Lubbock, Percy, 157

Macaulay, Thomas Babington, 50
McCarthy, Patrick J., 98n
McPhee, John, 35, 49; *Coming into the Country*, 50; *Crofter and the Laird, The*, 49–50; *Levels of the Game*, 50
Madden, Lionel, 19
Mailer, Norman, 20, 21, 37, 49, 72, 75, 83, 132, 168, 173, 180; *Armies of the Night*, 34; *Executioner's Song, The*, 83n; *Miami and the Siege of Chicago*, 34; *Of a Fire on the Moon*, 34, 101–4, 128–29, 144–50, 180–88
Mammon, 87, 96n, 100, 106, 118
Maurice, Frederick Denison, 43–44n
Melvill, Henry, 68
Melville, Herman, 68
Millett, Kate, 83

Milton, John, 29 + n; *Lycidas*, 18n; *Paradise Lost*, 18n, 29, 97
Miyoshi, Masao, 167n
Monk, Samuel Holt, 74n
Montaigne, Michel de, 166–70, 173–74
Morris, John N., 178n

Nebuchadnezzar, 44
New Journalism, 21 + n, 35
Newman, John Henry, Cardinal, 19, 70, 177
Nicolson, Marjorie Hope, 74n
Nietzsche, Friedrich, 40
Nightingale, Florence, 190

Oedipus, 42–43
Omerod, Justice, 113
Ostrander, Gilman M., 56n

Panofsky, Erwin, 90n
Pater, Walter, 133
Peterloo riots, 45, 58, 82
Peterson, Linda H., 178n
Pike, James, 104–5
Pisgah Sight, 66–69, 142
Pope, Alexander, 54
Poston, Lawrence, 28, 29n
Poussin, Gaspar, 136–37, 168
Preyer, Robert, 22n
prophetic poetry, 29 + n, 30
prophets, Old Testament, 51, 54, 168; attack audience, 86; conservative, 24; extraordinary instructors, 24; forthspeakers, 24; influence sages, 23–24, 189; quadripartite pattern, 26–27, 77, 163; reformers, 24; stance of, 51; and symbolical grotesque, 76
  Individual books of the Bible: Daniel, 17, 42–44, 54, 58, 61; Ezekiel, 57; Habakkuk, 17; Hosea, 57, 61; Isaiah, 17, 18, 26, 54, 60, 64; Jeremiah, 17,

196

Library of Congress Cataloging-in-Publication Data

Landow, George P.
  Elegant Jeremiahs.

  Includes index.
  1. American prose literature—History and criticism. 2. Wisdom in literature. 3. Prophecies in literature. 4. English prose literature—19th
century—History and criticism. I. Title.
PS366.W58L3   1986   828'.08   86-47644
ISBN 0-8014-1905-0